For Reference

Not to be taken from this room

EARLY
WOMEN DIRECTORS

EARLY
WOMEN
DIRECTORS

Anthony Slide

SOUTH BRUNSWICK AND NEW YORK:

A. S. BARNES AND COMPANY
LONDON: THOMAS YOSELOFF LTD

A. S. Barnes and Co., Inc.
Cranbury, New Jersey 08512

Thomas Yoseloff Ltd
Magdalen House
136-148 Tooley Street
London SE1 2TT, England

Library of Congress Cataloging in Publication Data

Slide, Anthony.
Early women directors.

Bibliography: p.
1. Women moving-picture producers and directors—
United States—Biography. I. Title.
PN1998.A2S557   791.43′0233′0922 [B]   75-20603
ISBN 0-498-01701-X

PRINTED IN THE UNITED STATES OF AMERICA

CONTENTS

Acknowledgments
Introduction

1 Alice Guy Blaché   13
2 Lois Weber   34
3 The Universal Women   52
4 Margery Wilson   62
5 Mrs. Wallace Reid   73
6 Frances Marion   83
7 Dorothy Arzner   92
8 Other Women Directors   102

  Bibliography   117

Superior numbers in the text correspond to entries in the Bibliography

ACKNOWLEDGMENTS

The general research for this volume was undertaken at the library of the Academy of Motion Picture Arts and Sciences and at the Motion Picture Section of the Library of Congress. To the staffs of both organizations I express my thanks. What few films, directed by women, I was able to view were in the collections of William K. Everson and the Library of Congress.

I must give special thanks to the following for their personal reminiscences: Simone Blaché-Bolton, Ethel Grandin, Olga Petrova, Mrs. Wallace Reid, Adela Rogers St. Johns, Alice Terry, Gilbert Warrenton and Margery Wilson.

Adela Rogers St. Johns, one of the most influential magazine and newspaper writers of the silent era.

INTRODUCTION

The present striving by women to achieve their rightful place in all levels of society—a striving commonly referred to as Women's Lib.—has sparked a number of books and a deluge of articles on women in film, women's place in films and the film industry, and the image of women that the cinema has created. The careers of several women directors have been the subject of much analysis and discussion, most of it regrettably far too biased to be worthwhile.

This outpouring of words on women in films has ignored one period of film history—the early years. Few women writers seemed willing to undertake the research necessary to uncover the facts concerning women directors before the coming of sound. It was far easier to protest about discrimination against women than to accept that there were more women directors at work in the American film industry prior to 1920 than during any period of its history. It would almost seem that women's rightful place was in the home, cooking, and bringing up children, rather than researching film history in the Museum of Modern Art, the Library of Congress or the New York Public Library.

During the silent era, women might be said to have virtually controlled the film industry. The stars were all women—the number of male actors who achieved any real prominence may be counted on the fingers of one hand—and many such stars had their own independent producing companies. Not only major stars, such as Mary Pickford, Corinne Griffith, or Mabel Normand, but also relatively minor actresses like Leah Baird, Helen Gardner, Alla Nazimova and Olga Petrova boasted their own producing organizations. Certainly such companies might be managed by men, but if, say, Gloria Swanson chose Joseph P. Kennedy to manage her company, that in no way detracts from Ms. Swanson's integrity or power.

In the field of screen writing, women wielded tremendous power. In 1918 alone, some forty-four women were employed in the film industry as scenario writers. The top screen-writers of the silent era were Beulah Marie Dix, Frances Marion, Bess Meredyth and Anita Loos, women whose names are still widely known. Indeed two of them, Frances Marion and Anita Loos, have published highly acclaimed autobiographies in recent years, and Beulah Marie Dix has been the subject of a book by her daughter. How many male screen-writers from the silent era are remembered today? C. Gardner Sullivan, possibly, but is there really any other male worth recalling?

As far as filmgoers were concerned, their minds were manipulated by the fan magazines and their gossip writers, and, here again, it was a woman's world. Adela Rogers St. Johns, Ruth Waterbury, Hazel Simpson Naylor, Gladys Hall and Adele Whitely Fletcher not only wrote for, but edited the fan magazines of the silent era—never again would such women shape the tastes of a generation.

First National Pictures even published a newssheet, titled *Fashions and Fillers for Feminine Fans*. In it Constance Talmadge "wrote" on "Opportunities for Women in Motion Pictures." One issue was devoted to the work of Ruth Oelman, a location finder, who told Ms. Talmadge, "It is wonderfully interesting work, it brings you in contact with such a wide variety of people, and the satisfaction one feels when a location has been found, which will later help towards the success of some great picture, is unsurpassable." Another issue featured the publicity writer, represented by Beulah Livingstone, who thought "publicity is the coming game of women." As the person largely responsible for building up Norma Talmadge to stardom, Beulah Livingstone is an excellent example of what women accomplished in the film industry. In England, Billie Bristoe handled publicity for all the top British stars, both male and female.

Even on the technical side of film-making there were women. In the mid-teens there were at least three camerawomen, Dorothy Dunn, Grace Davison and Margaret Ordway, not to mention one female assistant director, Mrs. Edna G. Riley, and four female studio managers, Alexia Durant, Nellie Grant, Lillian Greenberger and Annie Marchant.

Never hoping or expecting to receive any credit were the countless women who cut films in the days before there were film editors. And, of course, there was Margaret Booth, who headed the editorial department at M-G-M for countless years, and even today is active in the film industry; she receives credit as supervising editor on *The Sunshine Boys*. Let us not forget the women who hand-painted each frame of a Pathecolor film, for they were contributing their share to the art of the cinema. There was, in the early 'teens, at least one female film sales representative. I doubt there are any today. The only aspect of film production in which I can find

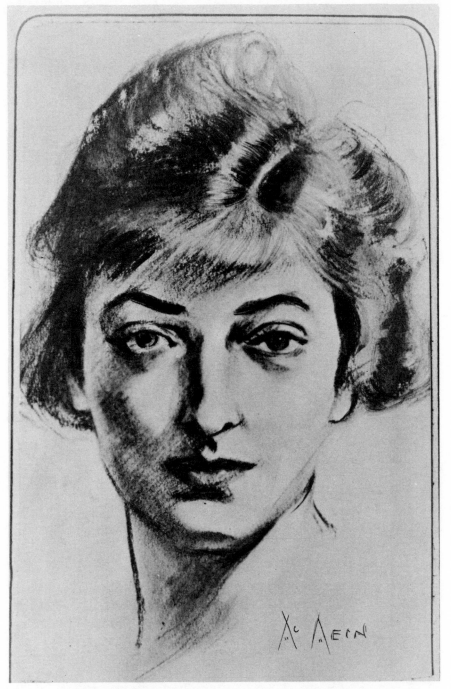

Beulah Livingstone, the silent screen's first woman publicist.

Thomas H. Ince's production of Hail the Woman, *directed in 1921 by John Griffith Wray, and featuring Florence Vidor and Lloyd Hughes, was one of the first women's liberation films.*

no record of female participation during the silent era is that of art direction.

Ethnic film production in the States also found a place for women in the silent era. The Mandarin Film Company, located, in 1917, in Oakland, California, boasted as its president, Marion E. Wong. The Company, which apparently produced at least one film, *The Curse of Quon Qwon*, was, according to *The Moving Picture World* of July 7, 1917, "the only Chinese producing concern in this country."

Women's predominant place in all areas of silent film production should be self-evident. As directors, women also left their mark on the silent film. Women directors were, quite obviously, not that unusual; a 1920 volume on careers for women devoted a full chapter to the woman film director. How many career guides for women today would offer even a paragraph for such a vocation? There were more than thirty women directors in the American film industry during the silent era, ranging from Alice Guy Blache, who must take credit for establishing that women could be film directors, to Dorothy Arzner, who carried over the tradition of the women film-makers into the sound era. Many of these women directors were the equal of, if not a little better than, their male colleagues. All of them, without a doubt, were pioneers in the true sense of the word.

"Women's chances of making a living have been increased by the rise of the cinematograph machines. Many a young actress anxiously awaiting an engagement will agree to this. At the start, when one concern controlled the production of moving pictures in this country, women helpers were not seriously considered in the plans of managers. As a rule when a woman was needed a man donned petticoats and played the part. Even now in a certain class of pictures this is sometimes done, but generally with pretty poor results. Every year there has been an increased demand for women to pose, and indications are that the demand will go on increasing, for, instead of one concern in the field, there are now fifteen at least.

We have no graded scale of pay, and the woman with a beautiful face gets no more than the plainer woman. Action, not looks, is what recommends a woman for employment with us, and the more experienced the applicant the better chance she has. Ingenues are not popular with managers and novices with no stage experience have no show at all."
—Views and Films Index, *October 3, 1908*

ALICE GUY BLACHÉ

Alice Guy Blaché was a true pioneer of the cinema. Not only was she the screen's first woman director, she was one of the first directors. *Photoplay* (March, 1912) described her as "a striking example of the modern woman in business who is doing a man's work. She is doing successfully what men are trying to do. She is succeeding in a line of work in which hundreds of men have failed."[1]

This remarkable woman was born at Saint-Mandé on the outskirts of Paris, into a comfortable middle-class family, on July 1, 1875.* In the mid 1890s, she was hired as a secretary by the French film pioneer, Léon Gaumont. At this time Gaumont was primarily concerned with the manufacture of motion picture cameras and projectors; the actual production of films did not concern him greatly. It was possibly this lack of interest which led him, early in 1896, to allow his secretary, Alice Guy, to write, photograph and direct, with the help of a friend, Yvonne Mugnier-Serand, a short titled *La Fée aux choux (The Cabbage Fairy)*.

Gaumont was pleased with the short, and Alice Guy found film-making enjoyable. She was, therefore, raised from the typical female occupation of secretary to the masculine one of film directing. Apparently, every motion picture produced by Gaumont until 1905 was directed by Alice Guy. In that year, needing additional assistance, Alice Guy hired Ferdinand Zecca as a director, Victorin Jasset as an assistant and Louis Feuillade as a writer. In so doing, it seems almost as if, with one mighty stroke, she had created the entire early French film industry.

In 1905, Léon Gaumont marketed the "Chronophone," which synchronized a projector with sound recorded on a wax cylinder. Yet again, it fell to Alice Guy to pioneer "talking pictures," of which she directed more than a hundred during 1906 and early 1907. Curiously,

*Most published sources list her year of birth as 1873, but Madama Blaché's daughter assures me it was 1875.

Alice Guy Blaché at the time of her marriage.

Alice Guy Blaché with Yvonne and Germaine Serand, the players in her first film, La Fée aux choux.

there appears to be doubt as to whether these early experimental films were successful. Certainly, it was not until December 27, 1910, that "Filmparlants" were demonstrated, satisfactorily, to the Académie des Sciences in Paris, "when Professor d'Arsonval had the unique pleasure of seeing and hearing himself making a speech before that august body of Savants."[*]

Herbert Blaché-Bolton, a Londoner, had come to the Gaumont studios to work as a cameraman, and to study French methods of film

[*]Proceedings of the Royal Institution of Great Britain, May 10, 1912.

One of Alice Guy Blache's early Gaumont productions, Triste fin d'un vieux savant.

Alice Guy Blaché's La vie du Christ *(1905)*.

Alice Guy Blaché outside her residence at Fort Lee, New Jersey.

Alice and Herbert Blaché with their daughter Simone in front of the partially constructed Solax studio at Fort Lee.

production for the early British film entrepreneur, Colonel Bromhead. Blaché-Bolton and Alice Guy fell in love, and became engaged on Christmas Day, 1906. Early in 1907, Léon Gaumont determined to open a New York office, and offered the position as its head to Blaché-Bolton. He accepted, and married Alice Guy only three days before they both sailed for the States.

The first thing the couple did on arrival in the United States was to drop the "Bolton" part of their name. From henceforth, they were to be known as Herbert and Alice Guy Blaché. For a short time, Alice Guy Blaché settled down to the life of a housewife; in 1908 she gave birth to a daughter, Simone. Then, in 1910, she determined to return to film production.

On September 7, 1910, Alice Guy Blaché established the Solax Company, with herself as president and director-in-chief. From 1910 through June, 1914, when Solax ceased to exist, Madame Blaché was to supervise the direction of every one of Solax's three hundred or so productions. The first, *A Child's Sacrifice*, was released on October 21, 1910, and featured "The Solax Kid" (Magda Foy).

Aside from Magda Foy, other players at Solax included Darwin Karr (who joined the company in November, 1911), Vinnie Burns, Marian Swayne, Blanche Cornwall, Claire Whitney, Billie Quirk, Lee Beggs, and Fraunie Fraunholz. The studios were at first located in Flushing, Long Island, but in September, 1912, new studios were completed at Fort Lee, New Jersey.

A description of Madame Blaché at the studio appeared in *Photoplay* magazine: "She quietly moves about the plant, unostentatiously and unobtrusively energetic. She carries with her an air of refinement and culture, and her dark, modest clothes bespeak and emphasize her dignity. This dignity, however, never borders on frigidity. She smiles encouragingly upon every one she meets. Her commands are executed to the letter with dispatch and efficiency, not because she is feared, but because she is liked. Although Madame has decided ideas, and at times will obstinately insist that they be carried out, she is always too willing to listen to suggestions. She is not a woman who is amenable to flattery. Unlike other women in business, she is really the first sometimes to see her own errors and will often, without resentment, admit the justice of criticism."[2]

In a letter to *Films in Review*, Frank Leon Smith recalled, "When I worked in the Pathe-Astra Studio in Jersey City her name [Alice Guy

Julia Hurley, Simone Blaché and Darwin Karr (heavily made-up) in Blood and Water, *released June 4, 1913.*

Blaché] was often spoken by my French bosses. They respected her, but, I think, also resented a woman succeeding as a writer, director, and producer of movies. One day I was sent to go over a script with a Pathe director working at Madame Blaché's glass-roofed Solax studio at Fort Lee. The big stage was empty at the time, and Madame Blaché was not there, but high on one wall, in letters two feet tall, was her mandate, 'Be Natural.' She had put this sign up for the guidance of the young and inept, self-conscious extras, and old pros (actors) addicted to stage tricks the camera could turn into farce, and it spoke to *me*, a confused young fellow—Her sign was amazing for those times, when the common phrase for acting in movies was 'posing for pictures.' "[3]

When Madame Blaché was otherwise engaged, her directorial duties were taken over by Edward Warren. Born in Boston in 1857, Warren joined Solax in the summer of 1911 after a lengthy stage career. He resigned from Solax in July of 1913 to direct a feature film on the Boy Scouts of America. From that point on, it was all downhill for Warren's career. By 1915, he was reduced to playing Douglas Fairbanks' valet in *The Lamb*. He died in Los Angeles on April 3, 1930.

It is difficult to determine exactly which films were directed by Warren and which by Madame Blaché. Certainly, Madame Blaché had overall supervision of all Solax productions. One of the first major releases of Solax, definitely directed by Alice Guy Blaché, was *The Violin Maker of Nuremberg* (released December 22, 1911). It was a tale of two apprentice violin-makers (Berkeley Barrington and Gladden James), who both loved their master's daughter (Blanche Cornwall). A violin-making competition is held to determine who will win the girl, but the better apprentice of the two, knowing that she really loves his rival, substitutes his violin for his competitor's. Of *The Violin Maker of Nuremberg*, *The Moving Picture World* (December 9, 1911) commented, "It is a story of tender sentiment told amid scenes of artistic quaintness. It carries a simple sentimental thread in a skillful manner that never descends to the commonplace, and, at the same time, holds the interest with its dignity and artistic charm." Incidentally, in a small role in this production, was Madame Blaché's daughter, Simone.

None of Madame Blaché's major Solax productions have survived, but some six one-reelers are preserved in the National Film Collection at the Library of Congress: *Greater Love Hath No Man* (released June 30, 1911), *The Detective's Dog* (released April 10, 1912), *Canned Harmony* (released October 9, 1912), *The Girl in the Armchair* (released December 13, 1912), *A House Divided* (released May 2, 1913) and *Matrimony's Speed Limit* (released June 11, 1913).

Vinnie Burns and Alice Guy Blaché with the star of Beasts of the Jungle, *released January 11, 1913.*

A viewing of these films reveals that Madame Blaché was demonstrating a remarkable sophistication in storytelling, *A Detective's Dog* is an amusing satire on early melodramas, with a dog racing to rescue its master, who is tied to a sawmill and about to be cut in half. In *A House Divided*, a married couple with domestic problems, of their own invention, adopt a policy of silence. *Matrimony's Speed Limit* is presumably based on the same David Belasco play, which was the source for Buster Keaton's *Seven Chances*, and involves a hero who must marry by a certain hour in order to come into an inheritance.

Solax productions by 1913 were released on an average of two-a-week. However, in October, 1913, Herbert Blaché founded Blaché Features—he had left the Gaumont organization a year earlier—and persuaded his wife to join him. Solax's last regular release was *The Rogues of Paris* on October 20, 1913. A few further films were released under the Solax label, but to all extents and purposes, Solax was no more.

The first release of Blaché Features—on November 17, 1913—was the four-reel, *The Star of India*, featuring Fraunie Fraunholz, Joseph Levering, and Claire Whitney, and directed by Herbert Blaché. It was not well received. *The New York Dramatic Mirror* (December 31, 1913) commented, "This is a four-reel melodramatic offering that staggers our credence. There is but one girl in the play, but the villains and the counter-villains and the hero as well, make the most of her that they can. The action around the girl entirely supercedes the quest of the Star of India—a valuable diamond—for over two reels, there being times when we almost forgot, and care less, about the whereabouts of that precious stone."

During its years of existence, approximately half of the productions of Blaché Features were directed by Madame Blaché. Blaché Features was followed by a new company, again promoted by Herbert Blaché, The U. S. Amusement Company, which released through Art Dramas. Most of the productions of the U. S. Amusement Company were directed by Herbert Blaché. A few, including *The Adventurer*, based on the novel by Upton Sinclair, and released on February 15, 1917, were directed by Madame Blaché. It is interesting to note her reputation as witnessed by this review in *The Moving Picture World* of March 24, 1917: "This reviewer has yet to see a picture by Madame Blaché that was not sincerely and artistically directed and this, *The Adventurer*, one of her recent productions is no exception."

During this period, Madame Blaché was chiefly employed by

Original poster for Dick Whittington and His Cat, *released March 1, 1913.*

Alice Guy Blaché.

Popular Plays and Players, a New York-based company, which released its productions through Alco, a subsidiary of Metro Pictures. She directed many of the features of the British-born dramatic actress, Madame Olga Petrova, including her first two films, *The Tigress* (1914) and *The Heart of a Painted Woman* (1915). Madame Petrova recalls of the other Madame in the early film industry:

Alice Guy Blaché was my first director in my first picture made under a contract for one film to be made by Popular Plays and Players. Mr. Lawrence Weber was its president. I believe the title was *The Tigress*. Mr. Aron Hoffman was the author.

I had met her and her husband, Mr. Herbert Blaché, at Mr. Weber's office. I liked them both but I was instinctively drawn to her. Had I been asked then Why? My answer would have been simple and direct, Why Not?

Knowing nothing of the methods of motion picture making, including directors, the idea of their sex did not occur to me. If it had I might have reasoned that Mr. Weber, being an astute business man, would not have risked losing the substantial profits he counted on me, a neophyte, if he had not recognized Madame Blaché a reliable, competent director, perfectly capable of protecting his interests. Anyway, I asked if she might direct me and was told she would be pleased to do so.

As I lived on Long Island, quite a distance from the studio at Fort Lee, New Jersey, which entailed ferrying my chauffeur, automobile and me across the Hudson River, 8.30 a.m. was fixed as my daily arrival there, subject to calls Mr. Lee Shubert might have for me under a contract. Work, not requiring me, however, was in progress much earlier. A few weeks later at 8.30 a.m. precisely, I reported at Fort Lee ready for initiation into the magic, mystery art and craft of the moving picture business.

Madame Blaché greeted me warmly. She introduced me to my co-workers of the day and to my cameraman by name. She showed me my dressing room. A vase of beautiful flowers welcomed me from the dressing table. She asked if I would like my lunch brought to me. She consulted me as to the menu and so on. In later days she would occasionally meet with me there for a little cup of black after-lunch coffee, and interesting, pleasant conversation.

These details having been attended to, Madame led me to the set. When the story had been sent to, and read by, me, I had voiced surprise that no dialogue and action were included in it. Mr. Weber assured me that all this would be meticulously attended to later. It was. But in no way did it resemble anything I could have imagined it would.

Instead Madame vocally outlined what each episode was about with words and action—pantomime—appropriate to the situation.

Of course, dialogue, pantomime as practiced in the theatre,

before audiences, individuals of which could see and hear from their various seats in the auditorium, was one thing, but to portray them before the single, uncompromising eye of the camera lens was quite a different proposition. This discomfitted me.

I noticed immediately that my co-workers wore a make-up much darker, almost a beige, whereas I wore the usual light Leichner's 1. This discomfitted me still further, but as Madame Blaché made no comment on it, neither did I.

I was shown the camera—or cameras. I had been photographed in private studios by professional photographic artists but these filled me with near terror. They appeared much taller, much bulkier than any I had seen, they seemed to resemble fearsome monsters from outer space. However—

Rehearsals started. In the first scene, as in all succeeding ones, Madame Blaché vocally outlined what each episode was about with action, words appropriate to the situation. If the first or second rehearsal pleased her, even though a player might intentionally, or not, alter her instructions, as long as they didn't hurt the scene, even possibly improve it, she would allow this to pass. If not she would rehearse and rehearse until they did before calling 'camera.' When she had cause to correct a player she would do this courteously, and in my case, which was more than often, she might resort to her native tongue. This gentle gesture touched me deeply, softened any embarrassment I might feel.

After all scenes set for the day had been shot the close-ups followed. These I found very difficult. The heat of the unguarded Kleig lights made one's eyes weep, one's skin burn, one's hair bristle. However they were part of one's obligation, and so had to be obeyed.

These concluded, Madame looked, and was, tired. But during rehearsals and shooting, she never lost dignity nor poise. She wore a silken glove, but she would have been perfectly capable of using a fist if she considered it necessary. She never bellowed through a megaphone as I was told many another director was wont to do. She obtained her results earning the respect and obedience of her artists. In the four succeeding pictures she never deviated from these methods.

Unfortunately I never met nor knew Madame, nor any of my co-workers, outside the studio. When work for the day was over, I hurried back to husband, home, and hearth as quickly as I could.

I suppose *The Tigress* pleased the public, and so Mr. Weber and Popular Plays and Players, since they offered me a contract covering a period of three years, albeit at a higher salary, and again subject to plans Mr. Shubert might have for me. Madame Blaché directed me in the first four under that aegis. They were, as I remember, *The Heart of a Painted Woman, My Madonna, What Will People Say* and a story, the name of which I don't remember, but was retitled as *The Vampire* for release. I am quite sure if the last named had come to me under that title I would never have been presumptuous enough to attempt to interpret it. The realm of the Vampire character had been created for and royally queened over by Theda Bara, and I would no more have attempted to emulate her in such roles than I would in those of an Ophelia either.

With the exception of *What Will People Say*, the play by Rupert Hughes, they were authored by Aron Hoffman. Why Madame Blaché didn't continue to direct me after those four I don't know, but I do know I missed her sorely. I only hope she found greener pastures. She probably did. Looking back again I retain for her the same reactions of deep affection and respect as I had for her so many years ago.

Bessie Love in The Great Adventure *(1918)*.

Also for Popular Plays and Players, Alice Guy Blaché directed other stars, including Doris Kenyon and Holbrook Blinn in *The Empress*, released on March 11, 1917. Commented *The New York Dramatic Mirror* (March 3, 1917), "The direction of this picture done by Madame Blaché further establishes her reputation as an able producer."

In the summer of 1917, Madame Blaché found time from her directing chores to give a series of lectures at Columbia University on filmmaking.

Alice Guy Blaché directs Bessie Love in The Great Adventure *(1918).*

Madame Blaché's last two films, both for Pathe release, were *The Great Adventure,* released on March 10, 1918 and *Tarnished Reputations,* released on March 14, 1920. The former was Bessie Love's first film for Pathe, and marked Flora Finch's return to the screen. It was Bessie Love's performance, which drew praise, as *Exhibitor's Trade Review* (March 2, 1918) noted, "It is her pleasing acting that pulls the rather unappealing story out of the rut and gives it the stamp of an accomplished production."

Tarnished Reputations featured Dolores Cassinelli, and was not too great a critical success. *Exhibitor's Trade Review* described it as "five reels of anguish." Commented Variety (April 9, 1920), "The story is by Leonce Perret and has a French melodramatic slant to it that is a little off the average of good American stuff. Mme. Alice Blaché directed. Neither of these experts are naturally adapted to bringing out in Miss Cassinelli those qualities that would put her at the top."

Madame Blaché was offered the direction of *Tarzan of the Apes,* but she declined that dubious honor. By 1922, she and her husband had separated, and Madame Blaché returned to France. In the late Twenties, she tried unsuccessfully to return to film production. She worked as a

29

A "liberated" Alice Guy Blaché smokes a cigarette.

translator, and attempted, yet again unsuccessfully, to sell a book for children, which she had both authored and illustrated.

She lived in France, Belgium and the States with her daughter, who had become a secretary in the American Foreign Service. Eventually Madame Blaché suffered a stroke; she died in New Jersey—the State in which she had spent virtually all of her years of filmmaking—on March 24, 1968.

Herbert Blaché continued as a director until the end of the silent

Dolores Cassinelli in Tarnished Reputations *(1920).*

era. In the late Twenties, he remarried, and by the early Thirties, he and his new wife, Helen, were managing a shop in Hollywood. Herbert Blaché died in Santa Monica, California, on October 23, 1953.

In the July 11, 1914 issue of *The Moving Picture World,* Alice Guy Blaché wrote a piece on "Woman's Place in Photoplay Production." It seems more than fitting to end this chapter on her work by quoting from that article:

31

Gladys Moon Jones sculpted Alice Guy Blaché while the director was living in Washington, D.C., in the Fifties.

It has long been a source of wonder to me that many women have not seized upon the wonderful opportunity offered to them by the motion picture art to make their way to fame and fortune as producers of photodramas. Of all the arts there is probably none in which they can make such splendid use of talents so much more natural to a woman that to a man and so necessary to its perfection.

There is no doubt in my mind that a woman's success in many lines of endeavor is still made very difficult by a strong prejudice against one of her sex doing work that has been done only by men for hundreds of years. Of course this prejudice is fast disappearing and there are many vocations in which it has not been present for a long time. In the arts of acting, music, painting and literature, woman has long held her place among the most successful workers, and when it is considered how vitally all of these arts enter into the production of motion pictures one wonders why the names of scores of women are not found among the successful creators of photodrama offerings.

There is nothing connected with the staging of a motion picture that a woman cannot do as easily as a man, and there is no reason why she cannot completely master every technicality of the art. The technique of the drama has been mastered by so many women that it is considered as much her field as a man's and its adaptation to picture work in no way removes it from her sphere. The technique of motion picture photography like the technique of the drama is fitted to a woman's activities.[4]

1. H. Z. Levine, "Madame Alice Blaché," *Photoplay* (March, 1912).

2. Ibid.

3. Frank Leon Smith, Letter in *Films in Review* (April, 1964).

4. Alice Blaché, "Woman's Place in Photoplay Production," *The Moving Picture World* (July 11, 1914).

2

LOIS WEBER

"When the history of the dramatic early development of motion pictures is written," noted *Motion Picture Magazine* in 1921, "Lois Weber will occupy a unique position. Associated with the work since its infancy, she has set a high pace in its growth, for not only is she a producer of some of the most interesting and notable productions we have had, but she writes her own stories and continuity, selects her casts, directs the pictures, plans to the minutest detail all the scenic effects, and, finally, titles, cuts and assembles the film. Few men have assumed such a responsibility."[1]

Lois Weber was, without a doubt, the most important woman director of the silent era. Not only do her productions stand equal with those of most of her male contemporaries, but virtually all of them display concerns, principles and beliefs which few directors, male or female, would have had the courage to place on film. I doubt that Lois Weber ever wrote or directed a film in whose subject matter she did not believe.

Her films took stands on a wide variety of controversial matters: *Where Are My Children* opposed abortion and advocated birth control. *The People vs. John Doe* was an indictment against capital punishment. *Hypocrites* attacked hypocrisy in our daily lives, in the church, politics, and in business. *The Jew's Christmas* dealt with racial prejudice.

Many Lois Weber productions concerned themselves with subjects in which she believed. Christian Science was glorified in *The Leper's Coat, Jewel* and its remake, *A Chapter in Her Life*. The underpayment of teachers and religious leaders was the subject matter of *The Blot*.

As early as 1913, Lois Weber spoke of her belief in films as a means of social change. In the course of a lecture, titled "The Making of Picture Plays that Will Have an Influence for Good on the Public Mind," before

34

Lois Weber in 1914.

the Woman's City Club of Los Angeles, she said: "During two years of church army work I had ample opportunity to regret the limited field any individual worker could embrace even by a life of strenuous endeavor. Meeting with many in that field who spoke strange tongues, I came suddenly to realize the blessing of a voiceless language to them. To carry out the idea of missionary pictures was difficult. To raise the standard was a different matter, but the better class of producers were prompt in trying to do this when they were brought to a realization of defects by

35

censorship. It took years to interest the best actors and to bring back refined audiences, but even this has been accomplished. We need thoughtful men and women to send us real criticisms and serious communications regarding our efforts."

Lois Weber was born in Allegheny, Pennsylvania. From early childhood she was interested in music, and it was this interest which led her to musical comedy. From musical comedy, she joined the Vance and Sullivan stock company, which specialized in melodrama. Here she met stage manager, Wendell Phillips Smalley, whom she married in Chicago in May of 1904.

Born in Brooklyn on August 7, 1875, Phillips Smalley was the grandson of Oliver Wendell Holmes, and the son of G. W. Smalley, New York correspondent of the London *Times*. He and his wife were to work together as a team until their divorce in the early Twenties. On most Lois Weber productions, Smalley is credited as co-director or advisory director, but it is obvious that he had little, creatively, to do with the films. The reason for the couple's separation is unknown, but as Adela Rogers St. Johns remarked to me, "male ego is a cause of a great many divorces," and it was probably the cause of this one. Smalley was not content to allow his wife the spotlight. Phillips Smalley ended his film career as a "bit" player, and died in Hollywood on May 2, 1939.

Finding it impossible to obtain engagements together on the stage, the couple decided to enter films. First, circa 1907, Lois Weber joined the Gaumont Talking Pictures Company. As she recalled some years later, "I wrote the story for the first picture, besides directing it and playing the lead. When Mr. Smalley returned [from tour] he joined me and we co-directed and played leads in a long list of films."[2] (It is interesting to note that both Lois Weber and Alice Guy Blaché worked as directors of early sound-on-cylinder "talkies.")

From Gaumont, the couple moved to Reliance, and then, in 1909, they joined Edwin S. Porter's newly formed Rex Company. With Porter, Lois Weber and Phillips Smalley helped write, edit, and direct all the releases of the Rex Company, aside from playing leads. In 1912, when Porter left to help form Famous Players, and the Rex Company became part of Universal, the Smalleys were placed in full charge of production.

The years with Universal were to prove the most important for Lois Weber. She and her husband would turn out during 1913 and 1914 two two-reelers a month; each short would be co-directed by them, feature the couple in the leading roles, and be written by Miss Weber. The couple had their own company of players, including Rupert Julian, Lule

Warrenton, Cleo Madison, Frank Lloyd, Elsie Jane Wilson, and Dorothy Davenport, all of whom were to become directors. Their cameraman was Dal Clawson, who was to remain with Lois Weber through 1921.

The Smalleys covered a wide range of topics in these Rex shorts for Universal. *His Brand*, released October 2, 1913, concerned a cowboy who brands his wife on the breast, and whose son is born with the mark of the brand. *The Jew's Christmas*, released December 18, 1913, demonstrated how race prejudice was conquered by parental love. *The Leper's Coat*, released January 25, 1914, indicated that "science has

Phillips Smalley

proven that fear of disease will produce its symptoms more surely than contagion, and that thought governs the body." *The Career of Waterloo Peterson*, released May 10, 1914, was a comedy of studio life, in which many Universal personnel appeared.

A comedy was unusual for Lois Weber, for as *The Universal Weekly* (November 29, 1913) noted, "Miss Weber's plays are always thoughtful and thought-compelling, deeply understanding of human nature and soul-searching in their revelation of truth."

Without a doubt, Lois Weber was one of the most popular members of staff at the Universal studios. In the autumn of 1913, she was elected mayor of Universal City. Asked about her policies, she said, "I cannot go into detail, but I can say that cleanliness in municipal rule and cleanliness in picture making will be the basis of my endeavors." (Incidentally, Universal City's chief of police was also a woman: Stella Adams of the Nestor Comedy Company.)

In March of 1914, it was announced that Lois Weber and Phillips Smalley would direct independently of each other, but this does not appear to have been the case. Instead, autumn of 1914 saw the couple make a surprise move in quitting Universal and joining the Bosworth Company, a producing organization founded by actor Hobart Bosworth, which released through Paramount. The Smalleys remained with Bosworth until April, 1915, producing many four and five reel features, including *False Colors, It's No Laughing Matter, Sunshine Molly*, and *Hypocrites*.

Hypocrites created a considerable stir when it opened at New York's Longacre Theatre on January 20, 1915. The film had been ready for release by November of 1914, but Paramount was somewhat uneasy about its reception because it featured a nude girl as "The Naked Truth," who pointed out the hypocrisy in the world.

Needless to say, *Hypocrites* was a tremendous success. "After seeing it, you can't forget the name of Lois Weber," commented *Variety* (November 6, 1914), "There is no other picture like it, there has been no other, and it will attract anywhere." The Ohio Board of Censors banned the film, and the Mayor of Boston demanded the clothes be hand-painted on "The Naked Truth," frame by frame.

The male dual lead of the monk who sees the hypocrisy of the world and the minister stoned to death by his congregation for unveiling a statue of "The Naked Truth" was played by Courtenay Foote. There is a slight mystery concerning the identity of "The Naked Truth." Some contemporary sources state she is portrayed by an actress named Margaret Edwards,

Courtenay Foote in Hypocrites *(1915).*

but I can find no record of such a player. Other sources claim that Lois Weber, herself, played the role, and there is quite definitely a resemblance between the director and "The Naked Truth."

Lois Weber returned to Universal with a reputation as one of the screen's most noted, and notorious, directors. Her first major Universal production was *Jewel*, based on a popular novel by Clara Louise Burnham, and featuring Ella Hall, whose publicity described her as "the darling of the films, the dearest little girl that God ever made," and Rupert Julian.

Jewel was the name of the heroine, who spreads love and happiness through her grandfather's home, with the aid of an unidentified book, which could only have been written by Mary Baker Eddy. "The story shows the delicate touch of their fair sex from curtain to curtain, handled and charged with simplicity," commented *Variety* (September 3, 1915).

The story of *Jewel* was obviously a favorite of Miss Weber. She remade it, in 1923, as *A Chapter in Her Life*. (The original novel was titled *Jewel; A Chapter in Her Life*.). The remake featured Claude Gillingwater and Jane Mercer, and is a delightful little program picture.

Jane Mercer and Jacqueline Gadsden in A Chapter in Her Life *(1923).*

40

Tyrone Power (center) in Where Are My Children *(1916)*.

Although not a practicing Christian Scientist, Lois Weber did attend the Christian Science church regularly, according to Adela Rogers St. Johns. Mrs. St. Johns cleared up the mystery of why the term Christian Science is never used in either *Jewel* or *A Chapter in Her Life*. Apparently the studios would not permit it. She recalls that she and King Vidor had to drop plans for a film dealing with Christian Science because of studio opposition.

Where Are My Children, which opened at New York's Globe Theatre in April of 1916 was possibly Lois Weber's most controversial film. Its subject matter was birth control; its basic argument was that birth control was a necessity and that abortion was a crime. Although the script for the film was by Lois Weber, it was based on an original story by Lucy Payton and Franklin Hall.

The film opens with two lengthy titles:

The question of birth control is now being generally discussed. All intelligent people know that birth control is a subject of serious public interest. Newspapers, magazines, and books have treated different phases of this question. Can a subject thus dealt with on the printed page be denied careful dramatization on the motion picture screen? The Universal Film Mfg. Company believes not.

The Universal Film Mfg. Company does believe, however, that the

41

A dramatic moment from Where Are My Children *(1916)*.

question of birth control should not be presented before children. In producing this picture the intention is to place a serious drama before adult audiences, to whom no suggestion of a fact of which they are ignorant is conveyed. It believes that children should not be admitted to see this picture unaccompanied by adults, but if you bring them it will do them an immeasurable amount of good.

Then followed a prologue of minor visual effect, showing the souls of little children in eternity, waiting to be born. The story proper concerned a district attorney (Tyrone Power), a great believer in eugenics, who learns he is childless because of his wife's visit to a doctor, illegally practicing abortion. After calling her a murderess, he forgives his wife, "but throughout the years with empty arms and guilty conscience she must face her husband's unspoken question, 'where are my children?' "

Where Are My Children was surprisingly well received. *The New York Dramatic Mirror* (April 22, 1916) commented, "It is not often that a subject as delicate as the one of which this picture treats us is handled as boldly yet, at the same time as inoffensively as is the case with this production. It succeeds in making its point, in being impressive, in driving home the lesson that it seeks to teach without being offensive. This is largely due to the capable direction of the Smalleys and the superb acting of Tyrone Power, aided by an excellent cast."

Anna Pavlova in The Dumb Girl of Portici *(1916).*

Another Lois Weber production opened at the same time as *Where Are My Children*, *The Dumb Girl of Portici*, featuring Anna Pavolva in her only screen role, supported by Rupert Julian and Douglas Gerrard. Miss Weber spent eight weeks in Chicago shooting, while Pavlova and her company were playing at the Midway Gardens. When Pavlova's Chicago engagement was over, she and Lois Weber came to Universal City for four further weeks of day and night shooting.

The finished film received mixed reviews. Julian Johnson, in *Photoplay* (April, 1916), wrote that "the brilliance, splendor and melodramatic power . . . are testimonials to the finest female imagination in filmland." *The New York Dramatic Mirrow* (April 15, 1916) was not quite so impressed. "Taken all in all, *The Dumb Girl of Portici* is a good spectacle, not so good as some that have been shown but still good enough to make its production well worth while."

Lois Weber returned to a controversial subject with *The People vs. John Doe*, which opened at the Broadway Theatre, New York, on December 10, 1916. This six-reel production told of a man, who, as a result of a third degree interrogation, confesses to a murder that he did not commit. "It is by far the most effective propaganda that has been seen in quite some time," commented *The New York Dramatic Mirror* of

The Dumb Girl of Portici *(1916)*.

December 23, 1916. The title of the production was changed, after release, to *God's Law*.

By 1917, Lois Weber had risen to the height of her fame. She was hailed as the screen's greatest woman director.[3] There was only one move that a woman of Lois Weber's talent and ability could make, and that was the formation of her own company with her own studio.

"For a long time it has been a dream of mine, as I suppose it has been of many another director, to have a company and studio of my own," said Lois Weber in an interview in the summer of 1917. "Now that dream is about to be realized, for I have the grounds; the stage is fast nearing completion and we are already in some of the buildings. And not only is it a complete and efficient studio but it will be the pleasantest to work in of any of the large number I have seen. We have taken a charming old estate here in Hollywood and converted it into our workshop. We have acres of ground, and shade trees and hedges and gardens, to say nothing of a tennis court. That may sound sentimental and feminine to many; but I am sure that we will make better pictures all the way round from having an inspiring and delightful environment in which to work."[4]

The headquarters of Lois Weber Productions was 4634 Santa Monica Boulevard, Hollywood. At this address, Lois Weber had not only her studio, but also her home. However, it was to be some time before the trademark of the Lois Weber Productions—an encircled Aladdin's lamp—was to appear on the screen, for the director was still under contract to Universal. While completing her contract there, Lois Weber leased her studio to Marshall Neilan Productions.

At Universal Lois Weber directed some six features—*The Price of a Good Time* (1917), *The Doctor and the Woman* (1918), *For Husbands Only* (1918), *Borrowed Clothes* (1918), *Home* (1919) and *Forbidden* (1919)—starring Mildred Harris, soon to become Mrs. Charles Chaplin. These films helped make Mildred Harris a star, whereupon she was signed up by a rising young film executive named Louis B. Mayer.

Lois Weber began shooting of her first independent production, *To Please One Woman*, in October of 1919. A reporter at the time asked her, "Whom are you going to direct?" "I don't know," she replied, "but of one thing I am certain—he or she won't be a star." Her choice of leading lady was a young actress from Olathe, Kansas, Clara Viola Cronk. Lois Weber renamed her Claire Windsor.

"Claire came to me directly from playing extra in an Allan Dwan picture," recalled Miss Weber. "A friend saw her and brought her to me, believing she was the exact type I was looking for. When she came she

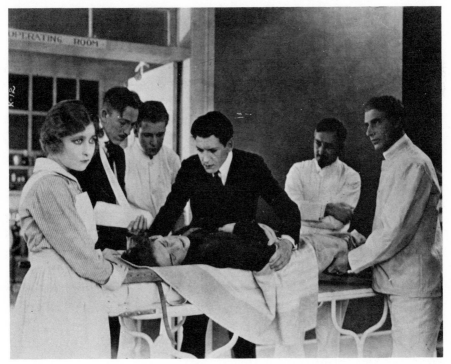

The Doctor and the Woman *(1918)*.

45

For Husbands Only *(1918)*.

didn't burst into a voluble recital of all she could do but stood quietly before me. It was like gazing into a mirror, I could read her very soul and I saw that she had great emotional and dramatic ability, with fine poise and possibility."[5]

Some six months or more were spent in the production of *To Please One Woman*, before it was finally released through Paramount on December 19, 1920. It was not an overwhelming success, critically or financially. The following review, written, incidentally, by a woman, from *The Moving Picture World* of December 18, 1920, gives a fair indication of the plot and the general critical response.

"Essentially a drama of human errors, Lois Weber's *To Please One Woman* shows how perverted womanhood brings unhappiness into the lives of many, causing the unwary to commit mistakes that result in their own ruin. The poison of this woman's selfishness infects almost everyone with whom she comes in contact. On account of her, her husband takes his life, the other man almost sacrifices the love of a good woman, a girl's heart is broken, and a young boy takes a dangerous ride that results in his death. Thus, the story has rather a doleful trend, and in its introduction of the deathbed scene of the boy-hero, is unnecessarily morbid. The acting during this emotional scene, and directly after, would be more effective if more restrained, and the whole would be more balanced if a saving scene of humor had left its trace here and there."

Lois Weber at work on a script.

Lois Weber directed only four further independent productions, all released during 1921: *What's Worth While, Too Wise Wives, The Blot*, and *What Do Men Want*. All featured Claire Windsor, supported by Louis Calhern (except for *What Do Men Want*). The features were not successful and reviews were generally unfavorable. Of *The Blot*, *Photoplay* (November, 1921) noted, "Typical Weber exaggeration, and rather tiresome."

Nothing it seemed could go right for Lois Weber. A writer in 1920 had commented upon the director's ability to combine an active working and domestic life. "Domestic hours are well interspersed in the life of Directress Weber and her efficiency behind the megaphone in the studio fails to interfere with her efficiency in her well ordered home. She declares that in the new woman we find the same woman known to the ages."[6] However, by the early Twenties, Lois Weber and Phillips Smalley had separated.

The bad reviews and the failure of her own company took their toll of Lois Weber. She lost faith in herself. There were reports that she attempted suicide. Despite her extraordinary career, Adela Rogers St. Johns remembers that she never seemed very dynamic. It was not until she was remarried—to Captain Harry Gantz—that Lois Weber felt able to resume her career.

She returned to Universal, her old alma mater, to direct Billie Dove

Claire Windsor in The Blot *(1921)*.

The final scene in The Blot *between the professor's daughter and the minister*.

48

Claire Windsor and J. Frank Glendon in What Do Men Want? *(1921).*

in two features: *The Marriage Clause*, released September 12, 1926, and *Sensation Seekers*, released March 20, 1927.

Also at Universal, Lois Weber was invited to script and direct a film version of the Duncan Sisters' popular stage success, *Topsy and Eva*. However, the racist humor did not appeal to the liberal-thinking Lois Weber, and she quit the film and the studio, which had for so long been her whole life.

Cecil B. DeMille invited her to direct a film based loosely upon the life of Texas Guinan, and titled *The Angel of Broadway*. Released on October 3, 1927 by Pathe, the production, featuring DeMille contract star Leatrice Joy and May Robson, is interesting for its portrayal of the

Lois Weber.

Salvation Army. By 1927 times had changed and women directors were a curiosity in the film industry. In its hints for exploitation, *The Moving Picture World* (November 5, 1927) suggested, "Give the women a special play on the strength of the fact that the author, the star and the director are all women."

The Angel of Broadway was Lois Weber's last silent film. In 1930, it was reported that she was managing an apartment building in Los Angeles. She returned briefly to the limelight in 1934, with a campaign to introduce visual aids to teaching, "to supplant the blackboard with the camera."[7]

Also in 1934, Lois Weber directed one final film, *White Heat*, a drama set on an Hawaiian sugar plantation, produced by a poverty-row studio called Pinnacle, and featuring Virginia Cherrill and Mona Maris. "Among independent productions, this rates way up near the top of the division," commented *The Film Daily* (June 15, 1934). "It has been written and directed by those who quite obviously are familiar with the unusual background of the melodrama."

Leatrice Joy in The Angel of Broadway *(1927)*.

Lois Weber died, almost penniless, in Hollywood on November 13, 1939. Her funeral expenses were paid for by Frances Marion, to whom Lois Weber had given her first job in the film industry in 1914.

Carl Laemmle, years earlier, had voiced a tribute that might very well serve as Lois Weber's epitaph. "I would trust Miss Weber with any sum of money that she needed to make any picture that she wanted to make. I would be sure that she would bring it back. She knows the motion picture business as few people do and can drive herself as hard as anyone I have ever known.[8]

1. Alice Carter, "The Muse of the Reel," *Motion Picture Magazine* (March, 1921).

2. Ibid.

3. "The Greatest Woman Director," *Moving Picture Stories* (July 7, 1916).

4. Arthur Denison, "A Dream in Realization," *The Moving Picture World* (July 21, 1917).

5. Carter, "The Muse of the Reel."

6. "The Domestic Directress," *Motion Picture Magazine* (July, 1920).

7. Winifred Aydelotte, "The Little Red School House Becomes a Theatre," *Motion Picture Magazine* (March, 1934).

8. Ibid.

3

THE UNIVERSAL WOMEN

In his legendary biography of the founder of Universal Pictures, John Drinkwater wrote, "Laemmle also startled the trade by giving women commissions to direct his pictures. Lois Weber, the most famous of them, Ida May Park, and Cleo Madison, were among the pioneers of his revolutionary suffrage."[1]

Of all the studios in the 'teens, Carl Laemmle's Universal could boast the largest number of women directors on its payroll. Most other producers employed one, or at most two, women directors, Universal at one time had nine women directors at work on its lot.

Why so many women directors at work at Universal? I doubt the reason was Carl Laemmle's concern for women's rights. What seems the most sensible explanation is that the company had embarked on too heavy a shooting and release schedule. Having committed itself to a certain number of films a year, Universal found that it had an insufficient number of directors under contract. Rather than hire additional directors from outside at a heavy expense, it was far simpler to find new directors in the ranks of the studio's contract actors, screenwriters, and editors—and who dominated such ranks? Women.

Among the Universal actresses who became directors, one of the busiest was Cleo Madison. Born and educated in Bloomington, Illinois, Miss Madison had an extensive career on the stage and in vaudeville before joining Universal. She began directing late in 1915, first two-reel dramatic shorts and then features.

Cleo Madison directed and starred in two five-reel features for Universal. The first, *A Soul Enslaved*, was released on January 24, 1916.

Uncle Carl Laemmle—the mentor to many of the silent screen's women directors.

According to *The Moving Picture World* (January 15, 1916), "This five reel production goes deeply into the more vital problems of human relationship, picturing the manner in which two people who have transgressed finally find happiness in each other's love." In the second, *Her Bitter Cup*, released on April 17, 1916, Cleo Madison, according to *The Moving Picture World* (April 22, 1916), portrayed Rethna, "a girl raised in a sordid slum district. She nurses the sick and even steals for them. Later the elder son of the factory owner fancies her and fits her up in an apartment. The contrasts of life are pleasing here, but the relations of the girl with Harry Burke are not made clear. In fact, at this point a number of mixed motives and obscurities creep into the story. The crucifixion of the girl's body at the close seems revolting. The story is quite strong in some respects, but certain features seem to lack proper significance."

According to *The Moving Picture Weekly* (April 15, 1916), Cleo Madison's role in *Her Bitter Cup* was "one of the most exacting she has ever played and taxes her great powers as an emotional actress." *Her Bitter Cup* also contained scenes shot during a freak snow storm in Los Angeles, and coincidentally the first snow ever to fall on Universal City.

Cleo Madison directed and starred in a host of two-reelers during 1916; some—*The Guilty One, The Girl in Lower 9*, etc.—were codirected with William V. Mong.

According to *Photoplay*, Miss Madison was a firm believer in the rights of women. "With the lovely but militant Cleo at their head, the suffragettes could capture the vote for their sex and smash down the opposition as easily as shooting fish in a bucket. Cleo Madison is a womanly woman,—if she were otherwise she couldn't play sympathetic emotional roles as she does,—and yet she is so smart and businesslike that she makes most of the male population of Universal City look like debutantes when it comes right down to brass tacks and affairs."[2]

Cleo Madison's time as a director was all too short, as were her years as a star. By the Twenties, she was playing minor roles in minor films. In later years, she recalled for one of her fans, "I went into 'White collar' work about 1931 and am retired now. Just growing old. I am sending you several of my remnants of old pictures. Keep what you like and dispose of the rest as I have no need of them. The Silent Films! Those were the happy days." Cleo Madison died, alone and forgotten, in Burbank, California, on March 11, 1964.

Another Universal actress turned director was Ruth Stonehouse, who had been a popular leading lady with Essanay before joining the Carl Laemmle forces in 1916. She was born in Elkhart, Indiana, on October 24, 1894, and had been a professional dancer before entering the movies.

Ruth Stonehouse does not appear to have started directing until the spring of 1917. One of her first directorial assignments was a two-reel Victor comedy titled *Dorothy Dares*. According to a Universal publicist, Miss Stonehouse was never happier than when she was playing child roles and "experiencing the feelings of a little girl again." Such was Universal's excuse for her directing and starring in a series of Mary Ann

Ruth Stonehouse.

Kelly stores. She was certainly petite. As a contemporary writer commented, "It seems incredible that this delicate, dainty little creature could be so masterful as to dominate a band of fiery photoplayers."[3]

Like Cleo Madison, Ruth Stonehouse's years as a star were over by 1920. She continued to play character roles well into the sound era, and died in Los Angeles on May 12, 1941.

Lule Warrenton joined Universal as an actress, specializing in "mother" roles, in 1913, A buxom, middle-aged woman, Mrs. Warrenton had been on the stage all her life. In 1916, Universal decided, at the suggestion of one of its leading male directors, Otis Turner, that she should direct a series of children's shorts, featuring child actresses Clara Horton and the Black Ernestine Jones; the first of such films was titled *The Calling of Lindy*. As was customary at Universal, Mrs. Warrenton had her own company, which consisted of Allan Watt as her assistant director, and Nora Dempsey, Irma Sorter, and Benjamin Suslow as supporting players.

Early in 1917, Lule Warrenton left Universal to form her own company, the Frieder Film Corporation, with studios at Lankershim,

FIVE RIPPLING ROARING REELS OF LAUGHTER!

A Bubbling, Sparkling, altogether Unique Rendition of
Kate Douglas Wiggin's Celebrated Masterpiece, "The Birds' Christmas Carol,"

"A BIT O' HEAVEN"
IN FIVE PARTS

THE CAST:

CAROL BIRD	MARY LOUISE
Uncle Jack	Harold Skinner
Mrs. Bird	Ella Gilbert
Mr. Bird	Donald Watson
Elfrida, the nurse	Madeline Eastin
Brother Donald	Carl Miller
Mrs. Ruggles	Mary Talbot
And nine raggedy Ruggleses.	

Carol Bird, the angelic child of wealthy parents is an invalid whose contact with the big world is confined to her father, mother, her nurse Elfrida, her much beloved Uncle Jack now sojourning in distant lands, and nine raggedy members of the Ruggles family who live in the house in the rear. An occasional letter from Uncle Jack with a trinket from the tropics and the surreptitious visits of one or more of the Ruggles' brood constitute Carol's only diversions. She is more spiritual than earthly—gentle natured, cheerful and universally beloved.

As the Christmas season approaches, Carol busies herself with thoughts of those around her, and one day conceives the wonderful idea of inviting the nine youthful Ruggleses to the Christmas feast, notwithstanding the shudders of father Bird at the awful thought of "watching those children eat." To heighten the joyful anticipations which this resolve brings, arrives a letter from Uncle Jack who begs them to stretch the nest a trifle to let him in for the holidays.

Christmas morning is the scene of much activity in the Ruggles' household. Good Mrs. Ruggles greatly laments the absence of her spouse who will not be there to see their "children enterin' s'ciety" in the big Bird home. She borrows a pair of stockings for "Peory," frames the precious invitation, makes Sarah Maude, the eldest, give them all "such a washin' an' combin' an' dressin' as they never had before," makes a dress for tiny Larry out of her precious old

"Is this your best shirt?"   "No ma'm it's my other one."

Original publicity for A Bit O' Heaven *(1917)*.

California. *The Moving Picture World* of February 17, 1917 explained the reason behind her new company: "The big idea 'Mother' Warrenton has had ever since she quit directing pictures for Universal is to produce photoplays with children as actors for the most part, she plans to present the comedies and the tragedies and the dramas of childlife, just as they appear to the child mind. She has studied the proposition deeply, and believes that by writing her own scenarios and directing her own scenes, and supervising the entire production, she can produce photoplays that will be intensely interesting to both old and young, and entirely suitable for children."

The Frieder Corporation's first feature, written and directed by Mrs. Warrenton, was *A Bit O' Heaven*, adapted from the popular children's novel, *The Bird's Christmas Carol* by Kate Douglas Wiggin. It featured "the incomparable child prodigy" Mary Louise, with Harold Skinner, Ella Gilbert and "Nine Raggedy Ruggleses." It was extremely well received. *Exhibitor's Trade Review* (June 23, 1917) described it as "an unusually high-class production filled with charming originality. . . . While the theme is simple and devoid of complexities of plot, it has all the appealing charm of youthful pathos." *Motion Picture News* (July 7, 1917) announced that "a feast awaits the picturegoing public, man, woman, and child in this production."

However, the Frieder Film Corporation's first success was also its last. Two further features—*The Littlest Fugitive* and *Hop O' My Thumb*—were announced, but there is no indication that they were ever released, and the company disappeared from view. In September of 1917, Lule Warrenton was back with Universal—as an acress.

Lule Warrenton continued to act until 1922, when she decided it was time for a rest. For a middle-aged woman, she had had a strenuous career in the film industry, not only as an actress and director, but also as founder of the Hollywood Girls' Club. She retired to her avocado ranch near Carlsbad, and died there on May 14, 1932. Her son, Gilbert, became a successful cameraman.

Grace Cunard and Francis Ford (brother of director John) were a popular starring team in Universal serials of the 'teens; their most famous being *The Broken Coin*, released during 1915. Aside from starring in these serials, Grace Cunard also wrote them and occasionally directed episodes. She also directed a number of shorts, sometimes in collaboration with Francis Ford, including *Lady Raffles Returns*, a feminist detective drama, *Born of the People*, and *The Terrors of War*. In 1914, she directed a burlesque of the civil war, titled *Sheridan's Pride*, released on March 4, and featuring Ernie Shields as General Sheridan. Grace Cunard was still remembered with affection by serial enthusiasts when she died, at the age of seventy-three, on January 19, 1967.

In the summer of 1914, Ruper Julian and his wife, Elsie Jane Wilson, a New Zealander by birth, joined the Universal Rex Company as actors, working under director Joseph de Grasse. Julian was eventually to become an important Universal director—his best known film was undoubtedly Lon Chaney's *The Phantom of the Opera* (1925)—after a period during the First World War when he was constantly required to impersonate the German Kaiser in films such as *The Kaiser–The Beast of Berlin*, which he also directed.

Elsie Jane Wilson turned to directing in 1917 with a series of pictures, featuring child actress, Zoe Rae. The films were, apparently,

57

Grace Cunard

not too inspiring. Of *My Little Boy*, released December 17, 1917, *The New York Dramatic Mirror* (December 15, 1917) wrote, "should recommend itself to audiences comprised for the most part of women and children. What parts of it that aren't dull are insipid." "A cheap feature at best," was *Variety*'s (November 23, 1917) opinion of *The Silent Lady*, released December 10, 1917.

Mrs. Julian preferred to leave the directing to her husband, and soon departed the film scene. She died in Los Angles on January 16, 1965.

Jeanie MacPherson.

After an early career in newspaper and publicity work, Ruth Ann Baldwin joined Universal as a writer; one of her first major assignments being the 1915 Herbert Rawlinson-Anna Little serial, *The Black Box*. In 1916, she assisted Lynn Reynolds with the direction of *End of the Rainbow*, featuring Myrtle Gonzalez. In the same year, she became a full-fledged director with her own company of players. One of her first films was *Retribution*, released on August 7, 1916, and featuring Cleo Madison. Announcing her appointment as a director, *Photoplay* (October, 1916) noted that "she has long been regarded as one of the most capable of Universal's staff."

Jeanie MacPherson is well remembered for her work as a scenarist for Cecil B. DeMille, for whom her first assignment was the 1915 Blanche

Sweet vehicle, *The Captive*. However, before joining DeMille, Miss MacPherson had been a director at Universal. Indeed, it was indirectly as a result of such directorial work that she came to join DeMille.

Miss MacPherson made her screen debut with the Biograph Company as an actress; from Biograph she went to the Edison Company, and from Edison to Universal, first as an actress, and then as a scenario writer. One of the first scripts she wrote, Miss MacPherson remembered in a 1916 interview as being *The Tarantula*, directed by Edwin August.[4] (Despite Miss MacPherson's describing *The Tarantula* as "the most popular and profitable film the company has produced," I can find no record of this title in any of the trade papers of the period.)

No sooner was the film completed than August left Universal. Unfortunately, the negative was accidentally destroyed, and, with the original director no longer at hand, Universal asked Jeanie MacPherson to reshoot it. Universal was, apparently, pleased with the result, and appointed Miss MacPherson both leading lady and director of one of the organization's producing companies, Powers.

Overwork led to nervous prostration; while recovering, Miss MacPherson met DeMille, who persuaded her to quit Universal. After devoting the rest of her life to the producer, Jeanie MacPherson died, in Hollywood, on August 26, 1946.

One of the most prominent Universal women directors of the later 'teens was Ida May Park; she even contributed a chapter on film directing to a 1920 volume on *Careers for Women*[5] Born in Los Angeles, Ida May Park went on the stage at the age of fifteen. It was in the theatre that she met her husband, fellow actor Joseph De Grasse.

When De Grasse joined Pathe as an actor, in 1909, his wife also entered films, not as an actress, but as a scenario writer. The couple joined Universal, in New York, during 1915, coming out to California in the spring of 1916. At Universal City, Mr. and Mrs. De Grasse worked together as a directing team, making as many as twelve features in eleven months.

In May, 1917, Ida May Park was given the opportunity to work as a solo director, handling one of Universal's biggest dramatic stars, Dorothy Phillips. Miss Park directed Dorothy Phillips in two major productions, *Fires of Rebellion*, released on July 2, 1917, and *The Grand Passion*, released on a States-Rights basis in January of 1918. The latter production also featured an actor destined for major stardom in the Twenties, Lon Chaney. *Fires of Rebellion* depicted "the sordid side of life as seen inside factory walls." Commented *Exhibitor's Trade Review* (July

7, 1917), "credit must be awarded Miss Park for the capable direction of the play."

Ida May Park talked at length on directing in a 1918 interview, published in *Photoplay* magazine:

> It was because directing seemed so utterly unsuited to a woman that I refused the first company offered me. I don't know why I looked at it in that way, either. A woman can bring to this work splendid enthusiasm and imagination; a natural love of detail and an intuitive knowledge of character. All of these are supposed to be feminine traits, and yet they are all necessary to the successful director. Of course, in order to put on a picture, a woman must have broadness of viewpoint, a sense of humor, and firmness of character—there are times when every director must be something of a martinet—but these characteristics are necessary to balance the others.
>
> It has been said that a woman worries over, loves, and works for, her convictions exactly as though they were her children. Consequently, her greatest danger is in taking them and herself too seriously.
>
> Directing is a recreation to me, and I want my people to do good work because of their regard for me and not because I browbeat them into it. . . . I believe in choosing distinct types and then seeing that the actor puts his own personality into his parts, instead of making every part in a picture reflect my personality.[6]

Ida May Park disappeared from the directing scene in 1920, for reasons unknown. Her husband continued to direct through the Twenties, and Ida May Park is credited as the writer of his 1926 production, *The Hidden Way*. She died, in California, on June 13, 1954.

1. John Drinkwater, *The Life and Adventures of Carl Laemmle* (New York: G. P. Putnam's Sons, 1931).

2. William M. Henry, "Cleo, the Craftswoman," *Photoplay* (January, 1916).

3. "The Directing Microbe," *Moving Picture Stories* (April 13, 1917).

4. Alice Martin, "From 'Wop' Parts to Bossing the Boss," *Photoplay* (October, 1916).

5. Ida May Park, "The Motion Picture Director," in *Careers for Women*, edited by Catherin Filene. (Boston: Houghton: Mifflin, 1920).

6. Frances Denton, "Lights! Ready! Quiet! Camera! Shoot!," *Photoplay* (February, 1918).

4

MARGERY WILSON

Today, Margery Wilson is remembered by film buffs as "Brown Eyes," the young bride-to-be who is murdered in the French Story from D. W. Griffith's *Intolerance*. Miss Wilson, herself, would probably prefer to be remembered for the many books which she has authored. One thing is certain, no one is likely to recall Margery Wilson, film director, but a film director she was, and a fairly good one from all accounts.

Margery Wilson was born, Sara Barker Strayer, in Gracey, Kentucky in 1898. At the age of eleven, she entered "show business." As she recalls, "I was considered a 'child wonder' at elocution—sometimes giving whole evenings of recitations. I was a 'Diseuse' at the age of eleven and twelve—going out from Sandy Valley Seminary (where my mother taught music, English, and drama) to give recitals for churches, clubs, etc. on a 50-50 basis. It came in most acceptably!"

At the age of fourteen, she obtained work as a leading lady with the John Lawrence Players in Cincinnati, Ohio. At the same time, rather than use her own name and bring disgrace on her family on account of her profession, she changed her name to Margery Wilson, because of her idolization of Woodrow Wilson's daughter, Margaret.

Late in 1914, Margery Wilson travelled down to Los Angeles from Seattle, where she and her sister had been appearing in musical comedy, to investigate the possibility of obtaining work for her sister in the film industry. As luck would have it, the first film company that Miss Wilson approached was Reliance-Mutual, of which D. W. Griffith was director-in-chief, and instead of signing her sister, the company hired Margery.

Margery Wilson in 1917.

D. W. Griffith originally intended in *Intolerance* for Miss Wilson to portray St. Veronica, the young mother whose dead baby Christ brings back to life, while en route to His Crucifixion. The director also had another role planned for the actress, in the Babylonian sequence of his production, as Margery Wilson recalled in 1919, "I was to be a slave in the market-place who was a conscientious objector. But alas, Mr. Griffith cut out the whole series and the poor slave never got a chance to object."[1]

Margery Wilson eventually essayed the part of "Brown Eyes" in the French Story of Intolerance, which dealt with the massacre of the Huguenots. Playing opposite her was a young actor named Eugene Pallette, who was to gain great popularity as a character actor in Hollywood films of the Thirties and Forties.

During the period she was under contract to Griffith, Margery Wilson would also appear in many non-Griffith directed Reliance-

Margery Wilson (seated far right next to Eugene Pallette) as most fans remember her as "Brown Eyes" in Intolerance.

Mutual features, including *Bred in the Bone* (1915 with Dorothy Gish) and *The Habit of Happiness* (1916 with Douglas Fairbanks).

While *Intolerance* was in production, Griffith would loan out the actress to producer Thomas H. Ince; her first Ince feature being the William S. Hart vehicle, *The Primal Lure*, released on May 21, 1916. When Griffith realized that he would have no further use for her, because of his planned visit to Europe to commence shooting on *Hearts of the World*, in October, 1916 he arranged for her to be put under contract to Ince's Triangle-Kay Bee Company.

She played opposite William S. Hart in three further films: *The Gun Fighter* (1916), *The Desert Man* (1917), and *Wolf Lowry* (1917). Margery Wilson was also featured in a score of Triangle releases, including *The Eye of the Night* (1916 with William H. Thompson), *The Sin Ye Do* (1916 with Frank Keenan), *The Last of the Ingrahams* (1917 with William Desmond), and *The Hand at the Window* (1918 with Joe King).

Late in 1919, Miss Wilson left Triangle, and played leading roles for Paramount in *Venus in the East*, with Bryant Washburn, and for Pathe in *The House of Whispers*, with J. Warren Kerrigan. A few months later, Margery Wilson became a director.

Miss Wilson's first venture as both director and star was *That Something*, based on the 1915 book by W. W. Woodbridge, dedicated to the Rotary Clubs of the World. As the director explains, " 'That

Something' refers to that unnameable thing that makes of a man a success or a failure."

That Something was shot at the Robert Brunton Studios in Hollywood. Miss Wilson remembers, "When I went over to Mr. Brunton, who had handled all the sets, etc., for Thomas Ince—and that was where I met him—he had always been very friendly to me—he tried to discourage me from producing and directing. He said it would be bedlam, and that the actors and even the 'grips' would just do as they pleased. But when he saw that he couldn't move me, he began to cooperate. He fixed up existing sets for my story and made it all possible, still shaking his head and saying I would lose my shirt, break my heart, and my health, et al.

"The first day on the set I called everybody together and told them the story and what I expected of each of them. I didn't know that Mr. Brunton was eavesdropping. I told my group that if they had suggestions of any kind to give them to me *now* for after we started shooting I wanted not a single interruption. Everything went like clockwork—everybody was so interested we even forgot about lunch—but when we did go over to the commissary to eat Mr. Brunton came over to the table and silently extended his hand, which I shook gravely."

Although shot early in 1920, *That Something* was not released until the spring of 1921, and then by the E. P. Hermann Film Corporation, which had gained financial control of the production. "I lost control of that through interference," explains Miss Wilson. "I didn't lose control of the others; I had cut my teeth." *That Something* did, however, play at least one theatre in Los Angeles, The Victory, in May of 1920.*

The five-reel feature, starring Margery Wilson as Sarah Holmes and Charles Meredith as Edwin Drake, received favorable notices. *The Moving Picture World* (April 16, 1921) commented, "New Thought, Will Power, 'Pollyanaism' and a suggestion of *The Passing of the Third Floor Back* make up the ingredients of this production of the Hermann Film Corporation. Starting in a third class boarding house and the purlieus of the underworld the story is concerned with the rise to wealth and position of the orphan slavey and the down-and-outer through 'That Something' which is here shown as the power of 'I will' in the human soul. The story is a consistent one. The chief fault in the direction lies in the sameness of action, which tends to monotony. Otherwise the production is a creditable one of its class."

*see The Los Angeles Times, May 14, 1920

On July 3, 1920, *The Moving Picture World* reported that Margery Wilson had begun work on a series of two-reel comedies, which she had also written, again at the Brunton Studios. The first of these comedies, *Two of a Kind*, was completed in the late summer of 1920, and concerned two young boys who looked alike.

In case it should appear odd that Margery Wilson could have taken so easily to film direction, she explains, "What most film people did not know was that I had had considerable experience directing on the stage. I had my own stock company when I was sixteen years old! As I told in my autobiography, I put on long dresses at age fourteen—being tall—and got a job as leading lady with the John Lawrence Players in Cincinnati, Ohio. After two years he went South, and the managers of the theatres we played in Covington and Newport, Ky., suggested that as I was the 'backbone' of the company, that I just continue after Lawrence was gone! This I did—and made quite a bit of money. So I was accustomed to direction before I got to Hollywood. It seems incredible, but true—my whole life is incredible!"

Margery Wilson was to direct two other feature films, *The Offenders* and *Insinuation*. Miss Wilson, today, does not recall which film came first. She believes it was *The Offenders*, but that does not appear to have been released until 1924, whereas *Insinuation* was released in 1922. I suspect they were both shot at about the same time, particularly as Miss Wilson's co-star in both was Percy Holton, and both were photographed in Vermont.

The Offenders was written by Katherine Holmes, and apparently dealt with "a miracle of healing." In her autobiography, Miss Wilson recalls, "It consisted almost entirely of beautiful exterior shots and was better that it deserved to be, all things considered."[2]

Of *Insinuation*, which she also wrote, Miss Wilson remembers much more. She told me, "I was the first person who ever made a film— not the Italians, not *The Bicycle Thief*, but Margery Wilson was the first person to make a film without a studio, without a single set. I was the first person in the wide world to do that, and the name of the picture was *Insinuation*. I wrote it, and directed it, and produced it, and acted in it, and sold it. I made over fifty thousand dollars, which I thought was a million at the time, now it would be nothing.

"I had done this before the Italians had ever thought of it, so this credit should stay in America, and not travel across, because I did it. I never thought about making history. I was just trying to save money, and I didn't see any reason to build a set that was already there. This picture

The Offenders: *Katherine Holmes (white-haired woman), Percy Holton (kneeling), Margery Wilson and Bradley Barber (pointing).*

The Offenders: *Margery Wilson and Bradley Barber.*

The Offenders: *Margery Wilson and Percy Holton.*

The Offenders: *Margery Wilson (center) with (in the carriage) Katherine Holmes and Mrs. A. B. Chandler.*

A dramatic scene from Insinuation.

was made in Vermont, and I had a whole carload of Kleig lights, spot lights and all that sort of thing, and took up an electrician. I arranged that we could tap the line anywhere. I moved these lights right into the actual rooms and homes.

"I had theatre scenes there in Randolph, Vermont. I was the guest of the Chandlers; Colonel Chandler was the President of the Postal Telegraph Company, which was before your time. They told me to go ahead and make a film, and they would pay for it. I had the actors from New York. Oddly enough, I met most of the actors I thought we needed face-to-face walking down Broadway. I had Percy Holton, who played the crippled boy in *The Miracle Man*; he played my brother in this film. I didn't pay anyone by the week. I said, 'What will you do this picture for?' I said this to my cameraman, everyone on the picture. I went to the electric company, and made a deal with them for all the juice, electricity, that we would need for the entire film. These three or four men looked at me, and said would fifty dollars be too much. I had to look down and hang on the table. So, I paid them fifty dollars for all the electricity I needed for that film. What they meant, of course, was they were so pleased I was going to give Vermont all this advertising that they were practically giving it away. I did everything on a flat basis. I didn't dare do it any other way. I

69

Insinuation: *Bradley Barber, Margery Wilson and Percy Holton.*

made it in the wintertime, and the scenes were so incredibly beautiful, oh so beautiful. I showed the film four times in Randolph, and people came all four times. They would have come every night."[3]

As is the case with all of the productions, directed by Margery Wilson, no prints of *Insinuation* are known to have survived. A tremendous pity, as this was possibly her best film. *The Moving Picture World* (September 2, 1922) was particularly impressed by it. "It is absolutely refreshing to review a picture like *Insinuation*, whose real value and appeal lies, at the outset, in its naturalness and which does not have to rely upon artificiality or luxurious props to aid in the telling of the story. In reality, *Insinuation* is a page taken bodily from the book of life itself, in fact several pages, and the story they tell is natural, wholesome, and absolutely faithful in detail and delineation. The plot of the picture-story is laid amid magnificent mountain scenery that is even more beautiful when covered with a mantle of snow . . . . It is not too much to say, however, that in the last analysis *Insinuation* will be classified as among the top-notchers, and that the exhibitor who is fortunate enough to obtain it for his patrons not alone is going to be able to please those patrons, but is sure to add to his own reputation as a picker of the worth-while."

Margery Wilson in the Sixties.

Miss Wilson embarked on a lengthy personal appearance tour with *Insinuation*, lasting three years, throughout the States and Canada. She was particularly well received in Nova Scotia. *The Halifax Evening Mail* wrote of her, "Margery Wilson is enshrined in the hears of her Halifax admirers, not simply because she is a screen star, but just because she is plain Margery Wilson, gifted by nature with all the wonderful qualities which enable her to carry her audience spellbound with her through the narrative of love, sorrow, malice, and finally triumphant joy. *Insinuation* is a human story in which the star and each and every member of the supporting cast are distinctly human."

Marriage forced Margery Wilson's retirement from the screen. "I married a man who didn't want me to do anything." However, in the late Twenties, she embarked on a new career as an authoress, and in the years to come published many highly successful books, including *Your Personality—and God* (1938), *Make Up Your Mind* (1940), *The Woman You Want To Be* (1942), *How To Live Beyond Your Means* (1945) and *Believe in Yourself* (1949).

Margery Wilson now lives in semi-retirement in Los Angeles, a woman who can look back on successes in many careers—as an author, film star, beauty and charm expert, and film director.

1. Helen Morton, "Brains, Brown Eyes and Buttons," *Motion Picture Magazine* (March, 1919).

2. Margery Wilson, *I Found My Way* (Philadelphia: Lippincott, 1956).

3. Anthony Slide, "An Interview with Margery Wilson," *The Silent Picture* (Spring, 1973).

5

MRS. WALLACE REID

Dorothy Davenport, who became Mrs. Wallace Reid—a name, incidentally, which she used from her marriage to the present, and a name she is proud to bear—like many of her contemporaries was an astonishing woman. A leading lady during the cinema's infancy, Mrs. Reid became a highly competent director, producer, writer, and entrepreneur after the death of her husband.

She was born in Boston in 1895, the daughter of famous acting parents, Harry and Alice Davenport, and it was in her mother's company that Dorothy made her stage debut at the age of sixteen. Around the same time, she entered films with the Biograph Company, and by 1912 was being hailed as "one of the youngest, prettiest, classiest and most bewitching actresses appearing in motion pictures."[1]

Wallace Reid and Dorothy Davenport were married in Los Angeles on October 13, 1913, while both were working for Universal. Reid was already a fairly popular leading man as a result of his earlier work at the Vitagraph studios, but he became a star because of his portrayal of Jeff, the blacksmith, in D. W. Griffith's *The Birth of a Nation*. Jesse Lasky and Cecil B. DeMille saw him in the film, at its Los Angeles premiere, and signed him to a long-term contract. The actor became Paramount's biggest male star. He also, quite innocently as a result of an accident, became addicted to morphine, an addiction which was to kill him at the height of his fame on January 18, 1923; he was thirty-one years old. His wife recalled; for DeWitt Bodeen, "I had over nine wonderful years of the best with Wally. I wouldn't trade anything for them. Wally died very young—but he gave freely of the gifts of his youth. Most of all, he loved people, and the public responded in kind. He was much loved. He had so many talents—the gods were overly kind, but they also made him

73

Dorothy Davenport (Mrs. Wallace Reid) in 1924.

vulnerable, his own worst enemy, to compensate for their lavishness. He knew too much—and not enough."[2]

The tragedy of Wallace Reid's illness and death was directly responsible for Dorothy's new career in the film industry. Mrs. Wallace Reid undertook a fight against narcotics. She established the Wallace Reid Foundation Sanitarium in the Santa Monica Mountains, "for the cure of unfortunate drug addicts,"[3] and accepted an offer from producer Thomas H. Ince to make and star in an anti-narcotics film, *Human Wreckage*.

Released on January 17, 1923, *Human Wreckage* was produced in co-operation with the Los Angeles Bureau of Drug Addiction, and dedicated to Wallace Reid, as the opening title of the production stated, "In

Dorothy Davenport Reid and Bessie Love in Human Wreckage *(1923).*

humble tribute to the memory of A MAN who fought the leering curse of powdered death and, dying, was victorious."

The script by C. Gardner Sullivan was based on an original story, "Dope," by Will Lambert, and the production was directed by one of Ince's contract directors, John Griffith Wray. Even with such competent technicians as Sullivan and Wray involved, it is obvious that Mrs. Reid had much to do with the production. She told me, "I did a great deal of work on the script; the supervision, trying to keep it as realistic as possible. I thought it came out well. I thought it accomplished its purpose. It was not just a contribution to the picture business, but a contribution to a cause."

The story of *Human Wreckage* concerned an attorney (James Kirkwood), who, like Wallace Reid, accidentally becomes addicted to morphine. Only when his wife (Dorothy Reid) shows signs of becoming addicted does the attorney gain the moral strength to shake off the habit.

Despite its depressing theme, *Human Wreckage* was a success. *The Moving Picture World* (July 14, 1923) described it as "a picture that holds your attention and forcibly delivers its message." "Not a cheery story for the whole family," commented *Photoplay* (September, 1922), "and yet a picture that will probably do the old world a lot of good. The drug evil has never known so stiff a celluloid uppercut."

Dorothy Davenport Reid and James Kirkwood in Human Wreckage *(1923)*.

Of Mrs. Reid's performance as the attorney's wife, Ethel MacFarland, *The Moving Picture World* wrote, "her presence on the screen establishes a deep note of realism and sincerity of purpose and her work in the role of the devoted wife keeps ever before you her own experiences."

Mrs. Reid produced one further feature for Ince, *Broken Laws*, based on an original story by Adela Rogers St. Johns, which went into production on August 18, 1924, and was released on November 9, 1924. Her director on this film, in which Mrs. Reid was also starred, was Roy William Neill. *Broken Laws* was dedicated to the mothers of America, as a reminder that the foundation of all law and order is the home. It was an attack on neglectful parents, who indulged the whims of their children instead of simply giving them a good spanking. Commented *The Moving Picture World* (January 31, 1925) "It is a picture that children as well as parents should see and one that will impress and please . . . for it has the rare combination of being vastly entertaining, putting over a forceful lesson and making you think, and you will continue to think of it long after you have seen the picture."

In 1925, Mrs. Wallace Reid formed her own production company,

Dorothy Davenport Reid as Joan Allen in Broken Laws *(1924)*.

Dorothy Davenport Reid and Ramsey Wallace in Broken Laws *(1924)*.

and began work on *The Red Kimono*, adapted by Dorothy Arzner from an original story by Adela Rogers St. Johns. The direction was in the hands of Walter Lang—his first assignment as a director—with Mrs. Reid very much assisting. The film—a story of a young girl lured into prostitution—was a critical disaster.

The Red Kimono, because of its subject matter, might be a popular success, but notices were uniformly bad. *Variety* (February 3, 1926) commented, "Mrs. Reid or someone else may believe she is doing something for the fallen woman in turning out a picture of this sort, but the chances are that she will do tremendous harm to the picture industry as a whole and to herself in particular because she sponsors it by permitting it to continue—And as a little side information, pictures such as this, although not so well made, which were the Germans' dream of quick money from the screen, set the German film industry back ten years."

The New York Times (February 3, 1926) was particularly down on the production. "There have been a number of wretched pictures on Broadway during the last year, but none seem to have quite reached the low level of *The Red Kimono*, a production evidently intended to cause weeping, wailing, and gnashing of teeth. Possibly it might accomplish its purpose if the theatre doors were locked, but so long as one knows one can get out of the building, it is another matter."

Priscilla Bonner as Gabrielle Darley in The Red Kimono *(1925).*

However, as Priscilla Bonner, the star of *The Red Kimono*, recalled for me, Mrs. Reid had other problems with the film, aside from the reviews. "*The Red Kimono* was written by Adela Rogers St. Johns and it was a true story. It happened in St. Louis. The heroine, whose name was Gabrielle Darley, had married, and married well, and moved away from her early life. After the film was released, she went to a picture show one day, and saw *The Red Kimono*. Even her name was used! She went to an attorney, and she sued Mrs. Wallace Reid. She got every nickel Mrs. Reid had, including the Wally Reid home in West Hollywood. Of course, they didn't realize they should change the name of the girl, but it was such a dramatic story, and it was filmed exactly as it happened."[4]

Undaunted, Mrs. Reid continued her film work. On April 4, 1926 she released, through Associated Exhibitors, her second independent production, *The Earth Woman*, again directed by Walter Lang, and again starring Priscilla Bonner. Miss Bonner remembers that the film was "thrown together" very quickly, in an effort to reap the rewards from the popular success of *The Red Kimono*.

A lurid melodrama, *The Earth Woman* was dedicated to "the toilers of the soil, the homesteaders who struggled to conquer the wilderness." Although not as successful at the box-office as *The Red Kimono*, it was better received by the critics. *The Moving Picture World* (May 29, 1926) commented, "This rather drab and cheerless story has little of comedy relief, the appeal is concentrated on the forceful drama of elemental persons and passions and the production is marked by well-drawn and interesting characterizations admirably handled by an excellent cast."

For the next two years, Mrs. Reid returned to acting with leading roles in two minor productions of an equally minor producer, Gotham. In *The Satan Woman*, released August 1, 1927, she was directed by her old friend, Walter Lang. *Hellship Bronson*, released in May of 1928, had Mrs. Reid cast opposite Noah Beery, under the direction of Joseph Henabery.

Mrs. Wallace Reid Productions was resurrected in 1929 for *Linda*, the first film on which Mrs. Reid was credited as director. Released on April 1, 1929, *Linda* featured Warner Baxter, Helen Foster and Noah Beery in a tale of a young girl forced to marry against her will. Following production of *Linda*, and after some promotional work on a 1930 Sono-Art production, *The Dude Wrangler*, Mrs. Reid announced her retirement.

However, a woman such as Mrs. Wallace Reid could not be expected to retire permanently. As one writer put it, "retiring is not so easy

Mrs. Wallace Reid in 1935.

for a small dynamo with an idea per minute."[5] In 1933, she returned to the film industry, not to work for any of the major studios, but to direct, produce and write for a number of poverty-row companies.

Her first assignment was as co-director, with Melville Shyer, on a 1933 Willis Kent production titled *Sucker Money*. Of this feature, starring Mischa Auer, Phyllis Barrington and Ralph Lewis, *The Film Daily* (March 1, 1933) wrote, "There's plenty of action, suspense, thrills and good old-fashioned melodrama in this story showing up the mystic seance fakery, and the subject is one that can be exploited to good advantage."

In 1934, she directed two features—*The Road to Ruin* for True Life Photoplays and *The Woman Condemned* for Marcy Pictures. *The Road to Ruin*, co-directed again with Melville Shyer, was the classic tale of a young girl's moral downfall. Commented *The Film Daily* (February 21, 1934), "The old story of young girls following the primrose path is honestly and frankly handled, without any suggestive scenes. It is a frank presentation of the pitfalls of youth, and it whitewashes none of the characters. The results of their folly, ignorance and carelessness are pointed graphically for the moral."

Mrs. Reid took time out at the end of 1934 to talk about the role of women in the film industry: "The first thing a woman producer must do is take the sex out of executive work. Either men are too polite and spare her the truth, or they go to the other extreme and have no consideration for legitimate foibles."

When asked as to what a woman executive could do to defeat antagonism towards her, Mrs. Reid replied, "She can use the fact that she *is* a woman to motivate things. That is, to take deliberate advantage of the theory that women must have a certain consideration not accorded men. Then, it is up to her to follow through with what she has to give. She simply uses the feminine viewpoint for her *approach*, but she must go from there to masculine attack and execution.

Honeymoon Limited *(1935) marked the start of Mrs. Reid's long association with director Arthur Lubin.*

"Before this, my experience had been with my own money. What I said had to go. Now I must work that much harder to convince that my slant is sound. I believe it takes a woman to believe in a woman's motives, and every story intended for the screen should have a woman working on it at some stage, to convince the audience of women. Later, also, everything a man does on the screen is done to please a woman or women. Actors says to me, 'You tell me what you think in this scene.' Where, if they were asking a man, they would be more apt to say, 'Tell me what to do.' A man and a woman, working together on the story, can hit a better emotional angle. For instance, a man only knows that he gets fed up with a woman, but he doesn't know *why*. A woman, writing the story, has feminine vision into all the little irritations that cause it."[6]

In 1935, Mrs. Reid produced and co-wrote *Honeymoon Limited* for Monogram. It was directed by Arthur Lubin, with whom Mrs. Reid was to have a long association as a writer and assistant. Through the Fifties, she worked with Lubin; she helped write the Francis, the talking mule, series from 1950-1956, which Lubin produced for Universal.

Dorothy Davenport Reid now lives, in semiretirement, as she likes to call it, in North Hollywood. She is still willing to work, but, as she told me, "for the last couple of years, I am just being lazy. They were great fun days. I loved the business. It wasn't arduous; it was just fun."

1. "Dorothy Davenport," *The Universal Weekly* (September 28, 1912).

2. DeWitt Bodeen, "Wallace Reid," *Films in Review* (April, 1966).

3. "A Remarkable Monument to Wally Reid's Memory," *Photoplay* (September, 1924).

4. Anthony Slide, *The Idols of Silence* (South Brunswick and New York: A. S. Barnes and Co., Inc., 1976).

5. Ruth Rankin, "Mrs. Wally Reid Comes Back," *Shadowplay* (December, 1934).

6. *Ibid*.

6

FRANCES MARION

Frances Marion's contribution to the cinema has been considerable; she was undoubtedly one of the most important screenwriters of all time. She is a perfect example of just how important women once were in the film industry. A list of the fims which she scripted reads like a table of the screen's greatest productions: *Stella Maris* (1917), *Rebecca of Sunnybrook Farm* (1917), *Pollyanna* (1920), *Humoresque* (1920), *Secrets* (1924), *Graustark* (1925), *Stella Dallas* (1925), *The Scarlet Letter* (1926), *The Wind* (1928), *Anna Christie* (1930), *The Big House* (1930), *Min and Bill* (1930), *Dinner at Eight* (1933), *Camille* (1937)—the list is endless. Apart from D. W. Griffith, she worked for practically every major silent director; Maurice Tourneur, Frank Borzage, Victor Seastrom, Marshall Neilan, Allan Dwan, James Cruze, John Ford, etc.

Adela Rogers St. Johns has written of Frances Marion, "As a writer, she is unquestioned head of her profession, male and female, and the proof is in the pictures to which her name is signed, and in the box office returns on those pictures."[1]

But it is as a director that this book is concerned with Frances Marion, and as a director she was not one of the greatest, competent as she might have been. She directed only three features—*The Love Light*, *Just around the Corner* and *The Story of Love*—a number that may indicate that she had no real love for directing. Unfortunately, Frances Marion's autobiography, *Off with Their Heads!*, offers no indication of Miss Marion's thoughts on directing. As Gloria Swanson notes in her foreword to the book, "She tells us little enough about herself."[2]

Born, Frances Marion Owens, in San Francisco on November 18, 1890, Frances Marion entered the film industry through the encouragement of Lois Weber. Weber engaged Marion as an actress and script girl in 1914, and generally looked upon her as a protegée.

Frances Marion.

Frances Marion directed her first film, *Just around the Corner*, at the request of William Randolph Hearst, for his Cosmopolitan Company in 1920. She had already successfully scripted one film for Hearst, based on a Fannie Hurst novel, *Humoresque*, and no one opposed her choice of a second Hurst story for her directorial debut.

Featuring Margaret Seddon and Lewis Sargent, hardly two of the silent screen's most prominent players, *Just around the Corner* was not released, by Paramount, until December 11, 1921. It received reasonably favorable reviews. *The Moving Picture World* (January 24, 1922) commented:

> *Just around the Corner* is human drama, a warm, sympathetic study of the home life of an East Side family. Adapted by Frances Marion from Fannie Hurst's story about New York, and also directed by Miss

84

Sigrid Holmquist, Lewis Sargent, and Margaret Seddon in Just Around the Corner *(1921).*

Sigrid Holmquist and Edward Phillips in Just Around the Corner *(1921).*

Marion, its slight plot has been deftly stretched into a Cosmopolitan Production of feature length, with few obvious evidences of 'padding.' The picture has hardly a trace of melodrama, though several of the situations give promise of it, depending for its appeal upon characterization and heart interest rather than action. It succeeds in reaching the heart through its excellent acting, even continuity and faithful portrayal of typical incidents in the lives of poor people.

For her next directorial-cum-writing effort, *The Love* Light, Frances Marion was reunited with an old friend, Mary Pickford. Frances Marion had first worked with Pickford as an actress in *A Girl of Yesterday*, in 1915. The following year, she had written her first original scenario, *The Foundling*, and its star was Mary Pickford.

The Love Light was produced by Mary Pickford, and released by United Artists on January 9, 1921. Playing opposite Pickford was Frances Marion's second husband, clergyman-turned actor Fred Thomson, who had made his screen debut in *Just around the Corner*, and who was to become a popular cowboy star. Frances Marion recalled for DeWitt Bodeen that *The Love Light* "was a challenge in more ways than one. Mary had never been directed by a woman, and my story offered her a highly dramatic role."[3]

Pickford's dramatic performance—melodramatic might be a more suitable word—was what the critics noticed. Writing in *The Moving Picture World* (January 22, 1921), Louis Reeves Harrison commented:

> *The Love Light* is a play of adventure full of outward movement, yet motivated by love and tempered by humor, a romance verging on romantic tragedy. The story will excite unusual attention from the fact that Mary Pickford has made a departure in the interest of variety, a departure from ingenue roles of comedy, a change which many will welcome. . . . . Her support is one of great excellence, especially in the Italian types, and the atmosphere provided by Director Frances Marion leaves nothing to be desired in the way of artistic backgrounds.

Both *Just around the Corner* and *The Love Light* have been preserved, but neither are available for study at the present time.

Frances Marion directed only one further film, *The Song of Love*, in collaboration with Chester Franklin. Released on December 24, 1923, the production featured Norma Talmadge and Joseph Schildkraut. It was not one of Miss Talmadge's best films. As *The Moving Picture World* (January 19, 1924) pointed out, "while it provides entertainment above the average, it. . . . . is somewhat of a disappointment because of what we have learned to expect in Miss Talmadge's productions."

Fred Thomson as Joseph and Mary Pickford as Angela in The Love Light *(1921).*

Raymond Bloomer as Giovannia and Mary Pickford as Angela in The Love Light *(1921).*

Fred Thomson and Mary Pickford in The Love Light *(1921).*

Arthur Edmund Carew, Norma Talmadge, and Joseph Schildkraut in The Song of Love *(1923).*

The Song of Love: *Norma Talmadge and Arthur Edmund Carew.*

The Song of Love: *Arthur Edmund Carew and Norma Talmadge.*

Frances Marion in the Thirties.

It is interesting to note the power that women had in the film industry at this time. Frances Marion's last two films both featured women stars with their own producing companies, who had *carte blanche* as to story, director, and supporting players.

Frances Marion continued as a screenwriter until as late as 1940, when she scripted James Whale's *Green Hell* at Universal. She had seen many changes in the film industry, including the decline of female power. She told DeWitt Bodeen, "I don't think Hollywood will ever again be as glamorous, or as funny, or as tragic, as it was during the teens, the

90

twenties, and the thirties. But that's what everybody says about the past as he grows older and looks back on the days of his youth, when everything was new and exciting and beautiful. Was it really that way? Frankly, too often, all I can remember are the heartbreak and the hard work."[4]

On May 12, 1973, Frances Marion died in Los Angeles. In its obituary, *The New York Times* described her as the dean of Hollywood screenwriters.

In 1934, Frances Marion's close friend, Adela Rogers St. Johns wrote of her, "As a woman, she is a philanthropist, a patroness of young artists, and herself the most brilliant, versatile and accomplished person in Hollywood."[5] Frances Marion could have asked no better epitaph.

1. Ivan St. Johns, "Good-Bye to Another Tradition," *Photoplay* (March, 1927).

2. Frances Marion, *Off With Their Heads!* (New York: The Macmillan Company, 1972).

3. DeWitt Bodeen, "Frances Marion," *Films in Review* (February and March, 1969).

4. Ibid.

5. St. Johns, "Good-Bye to Another Tradition."

7

DOROTHY ARZNER

In 1928, as the era of the silent film was drawing to a close, the magazine *Close Up* noted, "Dorothy Arzner in her so-far brief career as a director has already won an established reputation and a following of discriminating admirers."[1] With the advent of sound, Ms. Arzner was to become a major film director, but as this volume is concerned only with early women directors my survey of her career will deal only with the silent films which she directed: *Fashions for Women, Ten Modern Commandments,* and *Get Your Man.*

Dorothy Arzner was born in San Francisco, California, on January 3, 1900, to an American father and a Scottish mother. Her father, Louis Arzner, ran the Hoffman Café in Los Angeles, which was famous for its German cooking, and a favorite meeting place for film people. Here, celebrities such as Charles Chaplin, William S. Hart, and Erich von Stroheim would gather in the evenings, and here Dorothy Arzner developed her fascination with the film industry.

At the end of the First World War, Ms. Arzner decided she would like a job in the movies, what job she was not certain. She went to see William de Mille, who gave her the task of typing scripts. As she told Adela Rogers St. Johns, "Sometimes, I think that pride is the greatest obstacle to success. A silly false pride, that keeps people from being willing to learn, from starting at the bottom no matter how far down it may be, and learning every step of the way up. When I went to work in a studio, I took my pride and made a nice little ball of it and threw it right out the window."[2]

Some six months after joining the Famous Players-Lasky Corporation, Arzner became a cutter, assigned to Realart. "I learned more about

Dorothy Arzner.

pictures in the cutting room than anywhere else," Ms. Arzner has said.[3]

Early in 1922, Arzner was asked to edit Fred Niblo's *Blood and Sand*, featuring Rudolph Valentino. (She also claims to have filmed part of the bullfight sequences.) James Cruze, who had known Arzner back in the Hoffman Café days, was impressed by her work on *Blood and Sand*, and asked her to edit his next production, *The Covered Wagon*. Arzner edited three further Cruze features, *Ruggles of Red Gap* (1923), *Merton of the Movies* (1924), and *Old Ironsides* (1926).

Einar Hanson and Esther Ralston in Fashions for Women *(1927).*

After completion of her work on *Old Ironsides*, Dorothy Arzner was offered the opportunity to write and direct a feature at Columbia, then a "Poverty Row" studio. However, when Paramount learned of her plans to leave the studio for whom she had worked off and on for some seven years to direct at such a lowly studio as Columbia, they were dismayed. There was only one way to make her stay, and that was to allow her to direct.

She was offered a minor production, *Fashions for Women*, which was designed as a vehicle for Esther Ralston, who had risen to stardom as a result of her portrayal of the mother, Mrs. Darling, in Herbert Brenon's film version of *Peter Pan*.

The film, basically a melodrama enlivened by a lengthy fashion show sequence, was a reasonable box-office success. *The Moving Picture World* (April 9, 1927) commented:

> The production is the first offering of Dorothy Arzner, Paramount's new woman director. She seems to have been over-eager [sic] to direct, and some of the scenes show this in their lack of spontaneity. The action is directed, rather than natural, but as a whole the novice has done well. She has produced a colorful back-

The fashion show from Fashions for Women *(1927)*.

Curiously the ten commandments from Ten Modern Commandments *are also an advert for Dorothy Arzner's next Paramount production.*

Jocelyn Lee as Sharon and Esther Ralston as Kitten in Ten Modern Commandments *(1927).*

Clara Bow as Nancy Worthington in Get Your Man *(1927).*

Clara Bow and Charles "Buddy" Rogers in Get Your Man *(1927).*

Three portraits of the most famous woman director of all time.

ground and introduced bales of charming frocks. Between dress and undress the play should please both sexes.

Said Ms. Arzner: "I never had any obstacles put in my way by the men in the business. They all tried to help me. Men actors never showed any prejudice against working with me. All the men who help— cameramen, who are so terribly important—assistants, property men, actors, everybody helped me."[4]

After completion of *Fashions for Women*, Arzner was asked to direct another Esther Ralston vehicle, *Ten Modern Commandments*, released on July 2, 1927. Describing this tale of a maid in a theatrical boarding house as "flashy," *The Moving Picture World* (July 27, 1927) noted, "the story is a bit thin as to plot, yet it is well laid out to get and hold attention, and is more true to the life than many backstage yarn."

Dorothy Arzner's final silent film, *Get Your Man*, released on December 7, 1927, featured Clara Bow, and was intended as a follow up to the star's immensely successful, *Hula*. It was amusing, but in no ways as good as its predecessor. Dorothy Arzner directed Clara Bow again in what was possibly the star's best sound film, *The Wild Party*, released in 1929.

The denouement from Get Your Man *with Charles "Buddy" Rogers, Clara Bow, Josef Swickard, Harvey Clarke, and Josephine Dunn.*

Among Ms. Arzner's fourteen sound films, the most famous are: *Merrily We Go to Hell* (1932), *Christopher Strong* (1933), *Nana* (1934), and *Dance, Girl, Dance* (1940). She directed her last film, *First Comes Conway*, for Columbia, in 1943. Since then, Ms. Arzner has busied herself with a variety of projects, including teaching film at UCLA and the making of a series of television commercials for Pepsi Cola. Dorothy Arzner now lives in Palm Springs, and can trully call herself a pioneer as Hollywood's first woman director of sound films.

1. "Hollywood Notes," *Close Up* (April, 1928).

2. Adela Rogers St. Johns, "Get Me Dorothy Arzner," *Silver Screen* (December, 1933).

3. Ibid.

4. Ibid.

8

OTHER WOMEN DIRECTORS

There were some film companies where women directors were never to be found during the silent era: M-G-M under Louis B. Mayer was a forbidden zone as far as women filmmakers were concerned. However, most other producing organizations—both large and small—found a place for at least one woman director on their payrolls.

Most of the early producing companies gave their leading ladies at least one opportunity to direct. At Kalem, Gene Gauntier was the company's leading lady—except for a short sojourn with Biograph in 1908—from its formation in 1907 until the winter of 1912, when she founded her own company, The Gene Gauntier Feature Players, and was responsible for the scenarios of the bulk of the Kalem productions. She directed one film, *Grandmother*, which she also wrote, released on July 13, 1910. According to *The Moving Picture World* (July 16, 1910), "The story centers around the escapades of the pampered son of a wealthy father who falls in love with a popular dancer years older than himself and who is only slightly amused at the young man's ardor." *Grandmother* featured Anne Schaeffer (in her first film role), James Vincent, and Mrs. Julia Hurley, "one of the most famous old ladies of the stage."

Kathlyn Williams was the leading lady with the Chicago-based Selig Company, and in 1914, she directed, wrote, and starred in a two-reel feature, *The Leopard's Foundling*, released on June 29. In an interview in *Feature Movie Magazine* (April 15, 1915), Miss Williams said, "Women can direct just as well as men, and in the manner of much of the planning they often have a keener artistic sense and more of an eye for detail—and often it is just one tiny thing, five feet of film maybe, that

Kathlyn Williams (far right) in The Leopard's Foundling.

quite spoils a picture, for it is always the little things that go wrong that one remembers." Surprisingly, Kathlyn Williams was never given another opportunity to direct.

The Edison Company released a considerable amount of publicity in the summer of 1915 concerning a four-reel production, *A Close Call*, that their leading lady, Miriam Nesbitt, was to direct, write, and star in. Miss Nesbitt visited San Diego, San Francisco, and the Panama Exposition to shoot footage, but there is no record that this film was ever released.

The Vitagraph Company's most famous leading lady, Florence Turner, never directed while with the company, but in the autumn of 1919, she did direct and star in a series of one-reel comedies at Universal. However, Vitagraph could boast at least three women directors.

The most important, undoubtedly, was Marguerite Bertsch, who for many years had been the head of Vitagraph's Scenario Department, and wrote many of the company's early productions, including *The Wreck* (1913), *Captain Alvarez* (1914), *A Million Bid* (1914), and *My Official Wife* (1916). Her first film, *The Law Decides*, released on May 1, 1916, and starring Donald Hall and Dorothy Kelly, she co-directed with a stalwart Vitagraph director, William P. S. Earle. Her first solo assignment as director was on *The Devil's Prize*, released on November 6, 1916, in which her stars were Antonio Moreno and Naomi Childers. *The*

Two stills from Marguerite Bertsch's first film, The Devil's Prize *(1916)*.

New York Dramatic Mirror (November 4, 1916) commented that "The direction [sic] has selected a good cast and made the story fairly alive."

Moving Picture Stories magazine asked Miss Bertsch how she felt the first time she stepped upon the studio floor. She replied, "Why, to be perfectly frank with you, I didn't feel at all. You know I never wrote a picture that I did not mentally direct. Every situation was as clear in my mind as though the film was already photographed." Aside from her

The Son of Wallingford *(1921), directed by Mr. and Mrs. George Randolph Chester.*

duties at Vitagraph, Marguerite Bertsch found time to author a volume on *How To Write for Moving Pictures*, published in 1917.[1]

Mrs. George Randolph Chester's chief contribution to film history was as a script writer on her husband's and other Vitagraph director's productions. However, she co-directed at least one film with her husband, *The Son of Wallingford*, starring Wilfrid North, and released by Vitagraph on October 30, 1921.

Lucille McVey was born in Sedalia, Missouri, on April 18, 1890, and had an extensive stage career before marrying Sidney Drew, and joining the Vitagraph Company in 1913 to co-star with him in a series of highly successful domestic comedies. In January, 1916, the couple moved to Metro, and continued to be tremendously popular with the film-going public until Drew's death on April 9, 1919. Mrs. Drew was responsible for the elaboration and construction of most of the comedies while the couple were at Vitagraph, and, on their move to Metro, also began directing. Frederick James Smith, writing in *Photoplay*, noted, "Just between ourselves, I give Mrs. Drew 75 per cent of the credit for the conception of the Drew comedies. That is, she is the team member who selects an idea and builds it."[2]

105

Mr. and Mrs. Sidney Drew.

After her husband's death, Mrs. Drew ceased to act, but continued to direct. Her most important production was undoubtedly the Alice Joyce vehicle, *Cousin Kate*, released by Vitagraph in January of 1921. Lucille McVey Drew died in Los Angeles on November 3, 1925.

Nell Shipman spent some years with Vitagraph in the 'teens as a writer and actress. She appears to have been quite a remarkable woman, making her first professional appearance as a soubrette in 1906 at the age of fourteen, and going on to become a dramatic actress, scriptwriter, novelist, and film director.

Her particular delight was the great outdoors, as typified by the Canadian wilderness, where she set many of her productions. All of Nell Shipman's films had a feel for nature and contained preachments for ecology, in the days long before ecology meant anything. Her most

Nell Shipman.

famous film was *Back to God's Country,* based on the popular book by James Oliver Curwood, and released on September 29, 1919. (It was remade—not by Shipman—in 1927.) Old-fashioned, quaint, and creaky by today's standards, it was obviously not too well oiled when it was first released. *Variety* (January 2, 1920) commented, "The picture is a meller of the real old-fashioned kind, and after reading the story and seeing the picture it seems that the James Oliver Curwood tales make better reading than they do screen material."

Paula Blackton, second wife of the co-founder of the Vitagraph

Alice Joyce as Kate Curtis in Cousin Kate *(1921)*.

Company, produced, in 1917, a series of one and two reel shorts, titled "Country Life series," nominally directed by her husband, but, possibly, chiefly her own work. In the same year, Paula did direct a five-reel feature, titled *The Littlest Scout*, which received little if any favorable response from the critics.

From January, 1914, Mabel Normand is said to have directed all productions in which she starred at Keystone. This assumption is based on the following report, which appeared in *The Moving Picture World* on December 13, 1913. "Mabel Normand, leading woman of the Keystone Co. since its inception, is in the future to direct every picture she acts in. This will undoubtedly make Keystone more popular than ever, and this will give Miss Normand the opportunity of injecting some of her comedy, which she has never had an opportunity to put over before." Since Chaplin joined Keystone at this time, Mabel Normand was nominally director of the early films in which they both appeared, until Chaplin, as he relates in his autobiography, rebelled.

As is fairly widely known, Lillian Gish directed one film, *Remodeling Her Husband*, released on June 13, 1920, and featuring her sister, Dorothy Gish. Miss Gish has written and spoken at length on the

Two stills from Nell Shipman's Back to God's Country, *shot in Canada, on the Kern River, and at the Brunton Studios in Los Angeles.*

109

Dorothy Gish with Mae Marsh's sister Mildred and her niece Leslie in a scene from Remodeling Her Husband *(1920).*

film's production in her own autobiography, *The Movies, Mr. Griffith and Me*,[3] and in this writer's *The Griffith Actresses*,[4] and there is little point in repeating her comments here.

Unfortunately, *Remodeling Her Husband* is now a lost film, and there is no way of accurately knowing how good it was. It certainly garnered mixed notices on its original release. "If it were not for the inimitable comedy of Miss [Dorothy] Gish the feature would be a sorry affair," commented *Variety* (June 11, 1920). *Exhibitor's Trade Review* (June 19, 1920) thought, "Lillian Gish's directorial task is performed in a fashion which gains for her much of the credit attending the picture's success. The continuity is good, the grouping skillful and smooth; swift action prevails throughout."

Julia Crawford Ivers is a mystery woman director. No biographical data is available on her in contemporary studio directories. She suddenly appears as a director in 1916 with *The Call of the Cumberland*, the second production of the Pallas Company, released by Paramount on January 24, 1916. Featuring Dustin Farnum and Myrtle Stedman, the film was well received. *The New York Dramatic Mirror* (February 5,

Dustin Farnum and Myrtle Stedman in The Call of the Cumberland, *directed in 1916 by Julia Crawford Ivers.*

1916) noted, "The story is absolutely natural and due to excellent directing its effectiveness is most impressive and the photography is well nigh perfect."

The director appears to have been under contract to Famous Players-Lasky as a screenwriter; she was responsible for many of the productions directed by William Desmond Taylor. Then, in 1923, she directed—for Famous Players-Lasky—*The White Flower*, a melodrama involving curses and volcanos, set in Hawaii, and starring Betty Compson and Edmund Lowe. Julia Crawford Ivers died in Los Angeles on May 8, 1930.

The Russian-born (June 4, 1879, at Yalta in the Crimea) actress, Alla Nazimova, formed Nazimova Productions in the early Twenties, a company responsible for two films, *A Doll's House* and *Salome*. Both productions were directed by Nazimova's husband, Charles Bryant, but many historians have claimed that Nazimova herself should have received directorial credit, despite the lack of evidence to support such a claim.

Certainly, Nazimova must have taken a supervisory interest in the

Betty Compson and Lily Philips in The White Flower *(1923).*

productions. Ethel Grandin, an actress whose husband, Ray Smallwood, directed Nazimova in *Camille* (1921) and other films, recalls the actress' working relationship with her director: "Ray and Nazimova used to scrap and fight. We'd go down to the beach Sunday and Saturday, and one time we'd fix the lunch and the next time she would bring the lunch. And they would scrap and argue, but they worked out the scenes where they would do it two ways. She liked that fighting, because everybody was 'Yes, Madame,' and 'No, Madame,' but Ray wasn't like that. It used to make me nervous when I was near them. It wasn't relaxing. Ray was very upset all the time—it made him nervous working with her."

A *Doll's House* was released by United Artists on February 12, 1922, with Alan Hale playing opposite the Russian actress. It is interesting to note that Nazimova made her American stage debut in Ibsen's *Hedda Gabler,* and had played Nora in *A Doll's House* many times on the stage. Following *A Doll's House* came *Salome,* released by Allied Producers and Distributors on February 15, 1923. Mitchell Lewis portrayed Herod and Nigel De Brulier played Jokaanan in this production which featured sets and costumes designed by Natacha Rambova, based on the designs of Aubrey Beardsley. Neither film was a success, and

Nazimova Productions soon passed into oblivion. Nazimova continued to act until her death in Los Angeles on July 13, 1945.

Another actress with claims to direction, although certainly not as famous as Nazimova, was Stella Razeto, who in the 1922 issue of the *Motion Picture Studio Directory* claimed to be co-director on every film made by her husband, Edward Le Saint.

Many of the women directing in the Twenties were screenwriters or playwrights. The most famous was Marion Fairfax, the wife of actor Tully Marshall, who had authored many plays, including *The Builders* (1907), *The Chaperon* (1908), *The Talker* (1912 and *A Modern Girl* (1914). Circa 1915, she entered the film industry as a screenwriter with Lasky, at the suggestion of director William C. de Mille.

During the Twenties, in between writing, supervising, and editing more than thirty features, Marion Fairfax found time to direct *The Lying Fool*, a curious production dealing with drug addiction, released by the short-lived American Releasing Corporation on March 26, 1922. As her stars, Miss Fairfax chose Noah Beery, Marjorie Daw, and her husband, Tully Marshall.

Another playwright, turned screenwriter, Jane Murfin, co-directed (with Justin H. McCloskey) one production, *Flapper Wives*, starring May Allison, and released by Selznick on February 27, 1924. May Tully, the

Edmund Lowe and Betty Compson in The White Flower *(1923).*

author of a number of undoubtedly second-rate plays, including *Mary's Ankle*, filmed by Thomas H. Ince in 1920, directed two films: *The Old Oaken Bucket* (1921) and *That Old Gang of Mine* (1925). Both productions are probably best forgotten. The scenarioist on a number of minor films, Lillian Ducey directed at least one feature, *Enemies of Children*, a silly melodrama starring Anna Q. Nilsson, released by Mammoth Pictures on December 13, 1923.

Marion Fairfax with the cast and crew of The Lying Truth *(1922). Seated, from left to right, are Marjorie Daw, Claire McDowell, Noah Beery, unidentified, Marion Fairfax, unidentified, Tully Marshall and Pat O'Malley.*

Among the one-shot directors were Vera McCord and Ruth Bryan Owen. Miss McCord produced and directed *The Good-Bad Wife*, a very minor film of 1920, featuring Sidney Mason and Dorothy Green. Ruth Bryan Owen wrote, directed and starred in an Eastern melodrama, titled *Once upon a Time*, which featured The Community Players of Cocoanut Grove, Florida. She has a better claim to fame as the daughter of William Jennings Bryan.

Alice Terry was one of the silent screen's most beautiful and regal stars, particularly in the productions of her husband, Rex Ingram. What is not generally known is that besides looking glamorous, Miss Terry was able to take over direction whenever her husband was feeling out-of-sorts, which would appear to be quite frequently. Miss Terry received no credit for this work, but she is credited as co-director on Rex Ingram's last production, *Baroud*, shot in North Africa, and released in the States in 1933 as *Love in Morocco*. I have Miss Terry's assurance that the bulk of the direction was undertaken by her.

Elizabeth Pickett is another forgotten woman director, who would appear to have been multi-talented. After graduation from Wellesley in 1918, she took charge of the family tobacco farm in Lexington, Kentucky. She next joined the publicity department of the American Red Cross, where she directed a series of propaganda films, and wrote eleven hundred of the fifteen hundred pages of *The History of the Red Cross*.

In 1923, she joined the Fox Film Corporation, and informed production chief Winfield Sheehan, "I want to write and direct my own pictures."[5] Sheehan, took her at her word, and sent her back to Kentucky to write and direct a two-reeler, *King of the Turf*. Apparently, John Ford saw the short, liked it, and used it as a basis for his *Kentucky Pride*, released on September 6, 1925, which Miss Pickett edited and titled.

King of the Turf was to be the first of the Fox Variety shorts series, of which Elizabeth Pickett became West Coast Supervisor, and of which she wrote and directed forty odd subjects. Aside from the Variety series, she titled and edited several Fox features, including *The Shamrock Handicap* (1926), *Marriage* (1927), and *Fleetwing* (1928). She also wrote the 1929 feature, *Redskin*, for Paramount.

By the late Twenties, women directors were becoming fewer and fewer on American productions. Only Dorothy Arzner made a succesful transition to sound. If women directors had any future at all it would appear to be in Europe, and especially in England, where in 1932 American silent star, Jacqueline Logan directed for British International Pictures, *Strictly Business*, starring Molly Lamont and Betty Amann, and famed novelist, Elinor Glynn, directed two features, *Knowing men* and *The Price of Things*, both shot in 1930 by the distinguished American cameraman, Charles Rosher.

The coming of sound really signified the fade-out for the woman director in the States. Not until the late Forties and the rise to fame of Ida Lupino was there to be any room for them in the film industry again, and not until the late Sixties was any serious consideration given to woman's place in the film industry. Even in the Seventies, a woman enters a film industry entirely controlled by men—the cinema of Lois Weber and Alice Guy Blaché seems a millenium away.

1. Marguerite Bertsch, *How To Write for Moving Pictures* (New York: George H Doran Company, 1917).

2. Frederick James Smith, "Seeking the Germ," *Photoplay* (September, 1917).

3. Lillian Gish, *The Movies, Mr. Griffith and Me* (Englewood Cliffs: Prentice-Hall, 1969).

4. Anthony Slide, *The Griffith Actresses* (South Brunswick and New York: A. S. Barnes and Co., Inc., 1973).

5. Tom Waller, "Elizabeth Pickett," *The Moving Picture World* (December 17, 1927).

BIBLIOGRAPHY

Aside from the periodical articles and publications listed below, the files of *The Moving Picture World, The Universal Weekly* (later titled *The Moving Picture Weekly*) and *Moving Picture Stories* proved invaluable.

Aydelotte, Winifred. "The Little Red School House Becomes a Theatre," *Motion Picture Magazine* (March, 1934).

Bertsch, Marguerite. *How To Write for Moving Pictures*. New York: George H. Doran Company, 1917.

Blaché, Alice. "Woman's Place in Photoplay Production," *The Moving Picture World* (July 11, 1914).

Black, Ernestine. "Lois Weber Smalley," *Overland* (September, 1916).

Bodeen, DeWitt. "Wallace Reid," *Films in Review* (April, 1966).

———. "Frances Marion," *Films in Review* (February and March, 1969).

Carter, Aline. "The Muse of the Reel, " *Motion Picture Magazine* (March, 1921).

"A Charming Directress," *Moving Picture Stories* (November 24, 1916).

Denison, Arthur. "A Dream in Realization," *The Moving Picture World* (July 21, 1917).

Denton, Frances. "Lights! Ready! Quiet! Camera! Shoot!," *Photoplay* (February, 1918).

"The Directing Microbe," *Moving Picture Stories* (April 13, 1917).

Dixon, A. J. "The Only Camera Woman," *Picture Play* (January 1, 1916).

"The Domestic Directress," *Motion Picture Magazine* (July, 1920).

"Dorothy Davenport," *The Universal Weekly* (September 28, 1912).

"Dorothy Davenport," *Moving Picture Stories* (January 3, 1913).

Drinkwater, John. *The Life and Adventures of Carl Laemmle*. New York: G. P. Putnam's Sons, 1931.

Feldman, Joseph and Harry. "Women Directors—Seem To Go More Often Than They Come," *Films in Review* (November, 1950).

Ford, Charles. "The First Female Producer," *Films in Review* (March, 1964).

Gauntier, Gene. *Blazing the Trail*. Unpublished manuscript in the library of the Museum of Modern Art.

Gish, Lillian. *The Movies, Mr. Griffith and Me*. Englewood Cliffs: Prentice-Hall, 1969.

Grau, Robert. "Filmdom's Wonder Girl," *Moving Picture Stories* (January 12, 1917).

"The Greatest Women Director," *Moving Picture Stories* (July 7, 1916).

Guy, Alice, "La Naissance du Cinéma," *Image et Son* (April, 1974).

Harrison, Louis Reeves. "Studio Saunterings," *The Moving Picture World* (June 15, 1912).

Henry, William M. "Cleo, the Craftswoman," *Photoplay* (January, 1916).

Henshaw, Richard. "Women Directors," *Film Comment* (November, 1972).

"Hollywood Notes," *Close Up* (April, 1928).

"How Twelve Famous Women Scenario Writers Succeeded," *Photoplay* (August, 1923).

"Ida May Park, Director," *The Moving Picture World* (July 14, 1917).

James, Arthur. "Drawing Straws with the Interesting Sidney Drews," *The Photo-Play Journal* (March, 1917).

Jordan, Orma. "Kentucky Babe," *Photoplay* (October, 1916).

Lacassin, Francis. "Out of Oblivion: Alice Guy Blaché," *Sight and Sound* (Summer, 1971).

Levine, H. Z. "Madame Alice Blaché," *Photoplay* (March, 1912).

"Lois Weber—Mrs. Phillips Smalley," *The Universal Weekly* (October 4, 1913).

"Lois Weber on Scripts," *The Moving Picture World* (October 19, 1912).

Lowrey, Caroline. *The First One Hundred Noted Men and Women of the Screen*. New York: Moffat, Yard, 1920.

MacDowell, Josephine. "Lois Weber Understands Girls," *Cinema Art* (January, 1927).

MacMahon, Henry. "Women Directors of Plays and Pictures," *Ladies Home Journal* (December, 1920).

"The Making of a Feature," *The Moving Picture World* (March 1, 1913).

Marion, Frances. *Off with Their Heads!* New York: The Macmillan Company, 1972.

Martin, Alice, "From 'Wop' Parts to Bossing the Boss," *Photoplay* (October, 1916).

Morton, Helen. "Brains, Brown Eyes and Buttons," *Motion Picture Magazine* (March, 1919).

Park, Ida May. "The Motion Picture Director," in *Careers for Women*, edited by Catherin Filene. Boston: Houghton Mifflin, 1920.

Peary, Gerald. "Dorothy Arzner," *Cinema* (No. 34).

Peltret, Elizabeth. "On the Lot with Lois Weber," *Photoplay* (October, 1917).

Pepper, Peter. "Lule Warrenton Becomes a Director," *The Moving Picture Weekly* (July 1, 1916).

Potamkin, Harry Alan. "The Woman as Film Director," *American Cinematographer* (January, 1932).

Rankin, Ruth. "Mrs. Wally Reid Comes Back," *Shadowplay* (December, 1934).

"A Remarkable Monument to Wally Reid's Memory," *Photoplay* (September, 1924).

Remont, Fritzi. "The Lady behind the Lens," *Motion Picture Magazine* (May, 1918).

"Ruth and Her House," *Photoplay* (September, 1917).

St. Johns, Adela Rogers. "Get Me Dorothy Arzner," *Silver Screen* (December, 1933).

———. "The One Genius in Pictures," *Silver Screen* (January, 1934).

St. Johns, Ivan. "Good-Bye to Another Tradition," *Photoplay* (March, 1927).

Slide, Anthony. *The Griffith Actresses*. South Brunswick and New York: A. S. Barnes and Co., Inc., 1973.

———. "An Interview with Margery Wilson," *The Silent Picture* (Spring, 1973).

———. "Forgotten Early Women Directors," *Films in Review* (March, 1974).

———. *The Idols of Silence*. South Brunswick and New York: A. S. Barnes and Co., Inc. 1976.

Smith, Frank Leon. Letter in *Films in Review* (April, 1964).

Smith, Frederick James, "Seeking the Germ," *Photoplay* (September, 1917).

Tully, Jim. "Frances Marion," *Vanity Fair* (January, 1927).

"Turning Out Masterpieces," *Moving Picture Stories* (January 12, 1917).

Van Loan, H. H. "Lois the Wizard," *Motion Picture Magazine* (July, 1916).

Waller, Tom. "Elizabeth Pickett," *The Moving Picture World* (December 17, 1927).

Weber, Lois. "How I Became a Motion Picture Director," *Static Flashes* (April 24, 1915).

Williamson, Alice. *Alice in Movieland*. New York: Appleton, 1928.

Wilson, Margery. *I Found My Way*. Philadelphia: Lippincott, 1956.

Woodside, J. B. "She Was Padded to Fame," *Photoplay* (December, 1917).

119